LOSGET

Losget Press
2018

The Words of Yemen Chen

by Yemen Chen
Illustrations by Amber Hupo

Editor: Sunboyu Wang
Fangyu Ren
Designer: Tiger Hupo

LOSGET
Losget Press
2018

Author: Yemen Chen
Illustrator: Amber Hupo
Editor: Sunboyu Wang
Fangyu Ren
Designer: Tiger Hupo

The Words of Yemen Chen 2018 English 1st Edition

ISBN13: 978-1-7328459-6-1
ISBN: 1-7328459-6-4
LCCN: 2018913594

Los Angeles: Losget Press, 2018
www.losget.com
E-mail: contact@losget.com

INTRODUCTION

The Words of Yemen Chen is a gathering of diverse thoughts regarding common topics of life, dream, human and nature. Each independent thought is formulated in a metaphoric manner and is paired up with an eye-catching illustration, reflecting astounding imagination and insights of the author.

Author Yemen Chen invites his readers to search for the meaning of life. With humorous yet profound philosophical messages, this book reveals the secrets of everyday life from a rather unique perspective. It articulates the unique language of the mind and makes you reevaluate the relationship between you and the world. The freshness and vitality of the author's insights challenge the fixed perspectives through which ordinary objects and people are often perceived.

There may be moments while reading the book that surprisingly offers readers a sudden epiphany. The book is truly life-changing and can help you to approach challenges in a different approach.

CONTENTS

A Bathtub........................5
A Blessed One.................6
A Clear Mind..................7
A Cup.............................8
A Fool.............................9
A Great Man.................10
A Hated One.................11
A River..........................12
A Saint 13
A Thinker 14
All the Books in the World............................15
Bad Habits......................16
Beauty............................17
Being Confusing............18
Being Different..............19
Being Filthy...................20
Being Graceful..............21
Being Magical...............22
Blind Conformity..........23
Brain..............................24
Breathing.......................25
Chatting........................26
Conceit..........................27
Conjoined Twins...........28
Covering Up..................29
Death.............................30
Degeneration.................31
Dependence...................32
Development.................33
Elevating.......................34
Falling Apart.................35
Fear and Tremble..........36
Fighting.........................37
Flattering.......................38
Footprints......................39
For the Show.................40
GAIN and LOSS...........41
Getting a House............42
Go with the Tide...........43
God...............................44
Having A Tail...............45
Heritage.........................46
Humans.........................47
Joy.................................48
Leisure Time.................49
Letting Go.....................50
Luxury...........................51
Make Up.......................52
Masking.........................53
Money...........................54
Mosquito Nets 55
Nobody Wishes.............56
One's Mind...................57
Owing...........................58
Pants.............................59
Pay off...........................60
Picking Up.....................61
Pleasant to the Ears........62
Politeness.......................63
Praising Each Other.......64
Pride.............................65
Puberty and Breast-Feeding Period......................66
Puffing...........................67
Receiving.......................68
Reining the Horse Near the Cliff.........................69
Rudeness........................70
Salves............................71
School............................72
Secret............................73
Seeing Others................74
Self................................75
Showing off..................76
Speaking........................77
Struggling......................78
Sweetness.......................79
Textbooks......................80
The Animals..................81
The Author...................82
The Beautiful Thing.......83
The Bothering...............84
The Consolation............85
The CONVERSATION............................86
The Courage..................87
The Crowd....................88
The Curse......................89
The Darkness................90
The Debate....................91
The Despair...................92
The Difference..............93
The Dress for the Face..94
The Expectations...........95
The Face........................96
The Flowers of Happiness...............................97
The Food 98
The Footprints..............99
The Freedom...............100
The Friends.................101
The Friendship............102
The Game...................103
The Geniuses...............104
The Glory....................105
The Gourmet..............106
The Greatness.............107
The Happiness............108
The Hospital...............109
The Justice..................110
The Kingdom..............111
The Kiss......................112
The Lessons................113
The Lord of Creations..114
The Neck....................115
The Nonsenses............116
The Ocean of Knowledge............................117
The Origin of Troubles118
The Ping-Pong Players119
The Precious Things....120
The Pride.....................121
The Redemption..........122
The Regrets.................123
The Responsibility........124
The Result...................125
The Reversed...............126
The Role......................127
The Same....................128
The Setbacks................129
The Sky Getting Dark..130
The Setbacks...............129
The Sky Getting Dark..130
The Speed...................131
The Starry Sky.............132
The Statue...................133
The Successes..............134
The Sympathy and Jealousy.................................135
The Talents.................136
The Things You Need..137
The Toothache............138
The Troubles...............139
The Truth...................140
The Tyrant..................141
The Unnerving Thing..142
The Vaulting Pole........143
The Wise Men............144
The Youth...................145
Time Flies....................146
To Be a Hermit...........147
To Be Strong...............148
To Betray.....................149
To Breathe...................150
To Control..................151
To Create....................152
To Distort...................153
To Forgive...................154
To Help.......................155
To Judge......................156
To Labor.....................157
To Lose.......................158
To Love or Hate..........159
To Rein.......................160
To Respect..................161
To See.........................162
To Speculate...............163
To Stay Silent..............164
To Think as A Thinker.................................165
To Waste.....................166
Traveling Round the World 167
Understanding.............168
Us................................169
Value...........................170
Vanity..........................171
WAITING..................172
With Food...................173

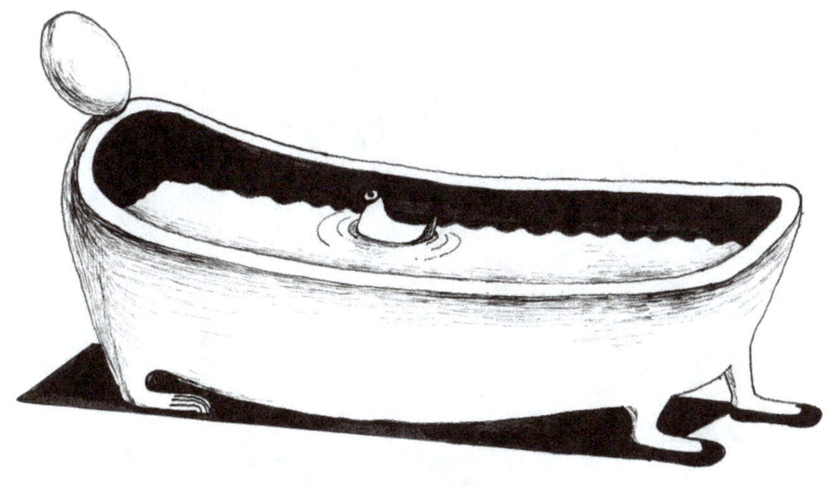

A BATHTUB

A bathtub is a place where people feel dirty in clean water and feel clean in dirty water.

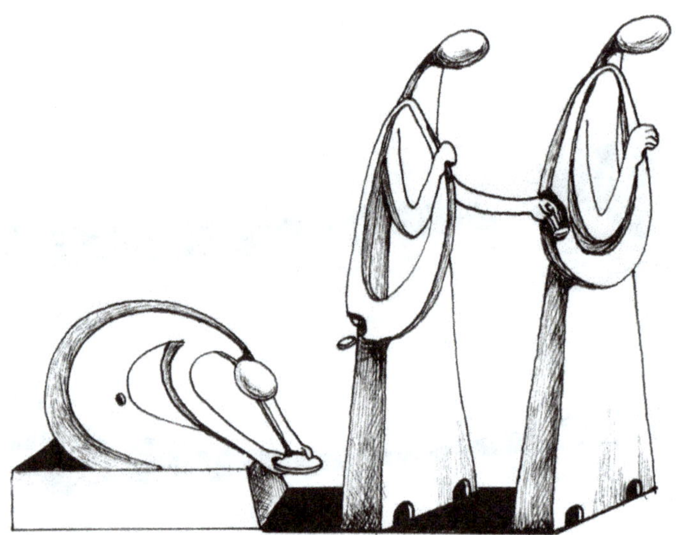

A BLESSED ONE

When a blessed one takes financial advantages of others, they lose the same amount in another business. However, an unblessed one often loses something more important.

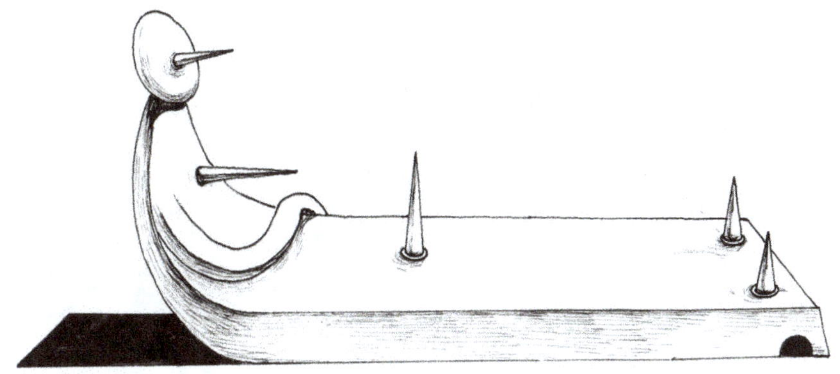

A CLEAR MIND

Sickness brings clarity to human minds. At that moment, human finally realize that being alive is already a blessing.

A CUP

People pour water into a cup to drink it. However, this action often makes the cup feel happy or sad along with the gains or losses.

A FOOL

Only do fools laugh at other fools. Wise men do not do that because they know for sure that they are the same kind.

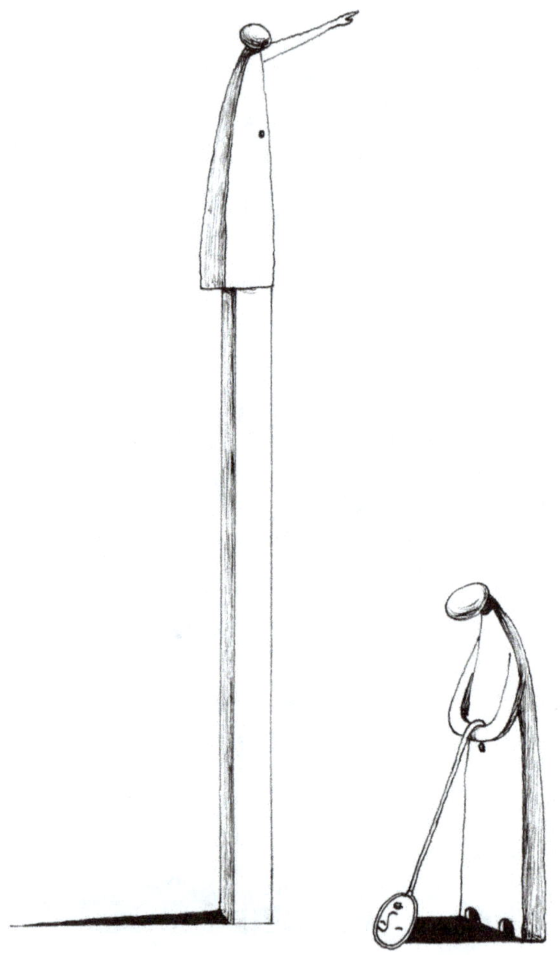

A GREAT MAN

A great man gives many people an impression that their lives will be wasted if they cannot become that kind of person. However, they truly waste their life due to this mindset.

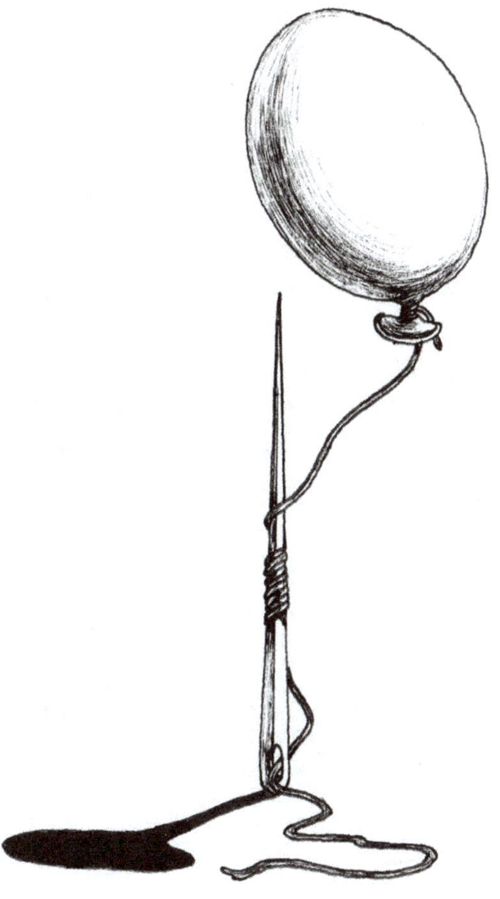

A HATED ONE

A lot of people's spiritual supports do not come from the loved ones but the hated ones. They just do not want to make any mistakes in front of them.

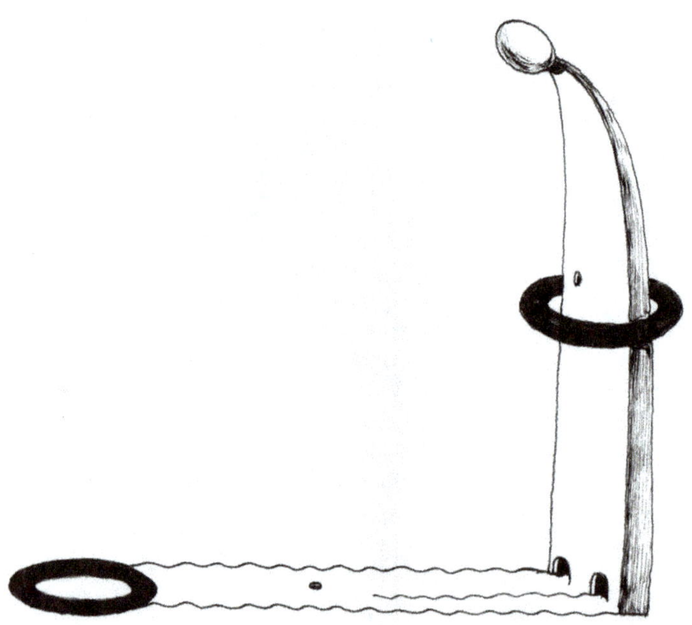

A RIVER

Time is a river that we drowned in as soon as we were born. All proceedings just lead to a full realization that we had actually drowned in it.

A SAINT

A saint must not be a saint if his reputation has never been denigrated.

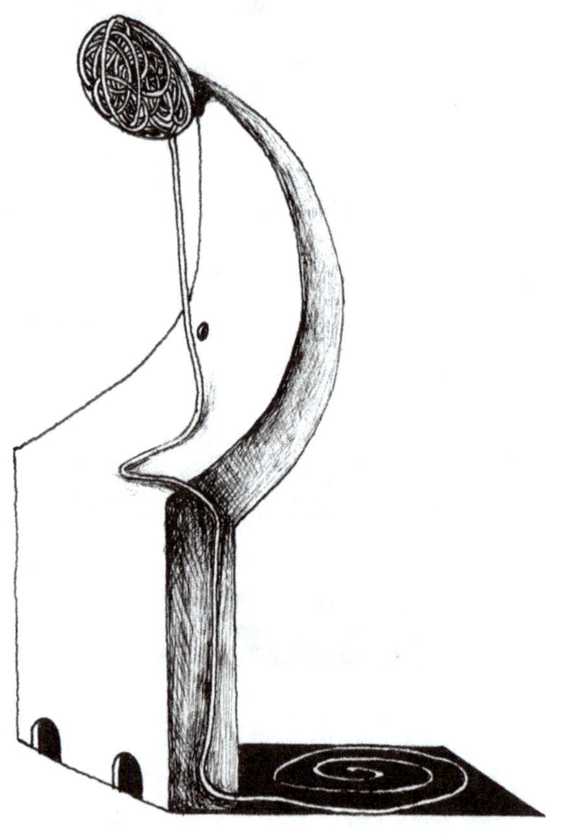

A THINKER

A true thinker cannot improve his circumstance through his thoughts.

ALL THE BOOKS IN THE WORLD

If you can cut all the fake, meaningless and useless words in the books, then I can fit all the books in the word into my pants pocket.

BAD HABITS

One of human's bad habits is that they are still obsessed with minor problems even they are already in great happiness.

BEAUTY

Beauty is the common enemy of women. It let them fall in love in it and then abandons them.

BEING CONFUSING

Marriage would considerably change the fates of the couples. It is nerve-wracking that both of them were confused when they made the decision.

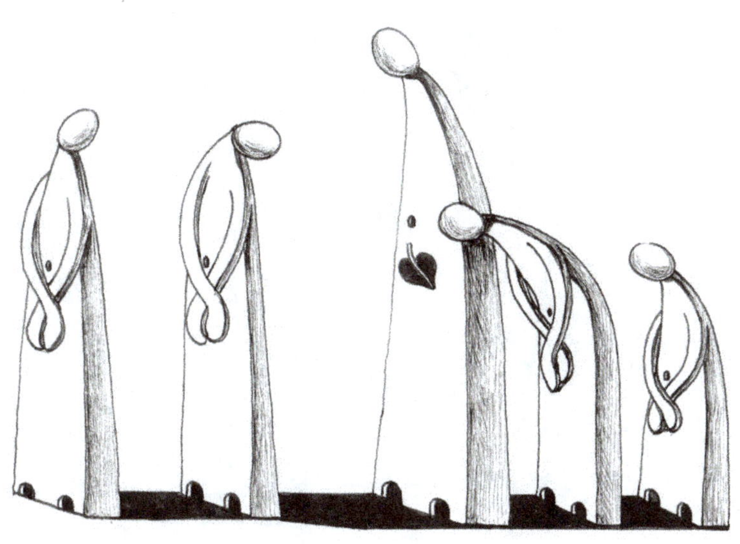

BEING DIFFERENT

When trapped in a crowd, a person is shameful for being different.

BEING FILTHY

Human beings are weird. After generating garbage, they think that people who clean them up are filthy.

BEING GRACEFUL

A graceful person must be lucky because he is not suffering from hunger at the moment.

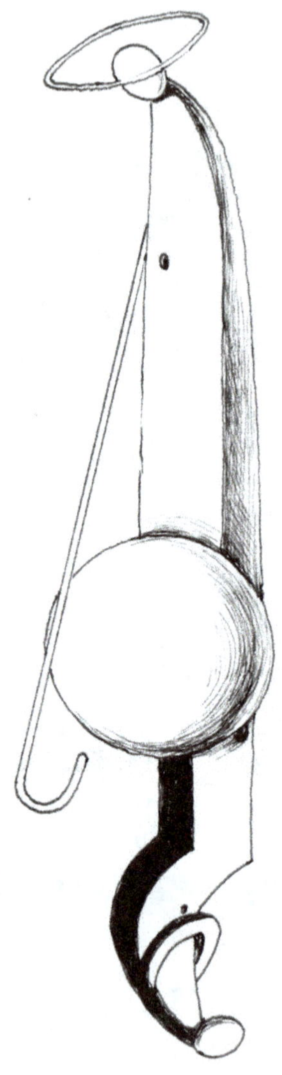

BEING MAGICAL

Flying is not magical but gravity is. Dreams are not magical but reality is.

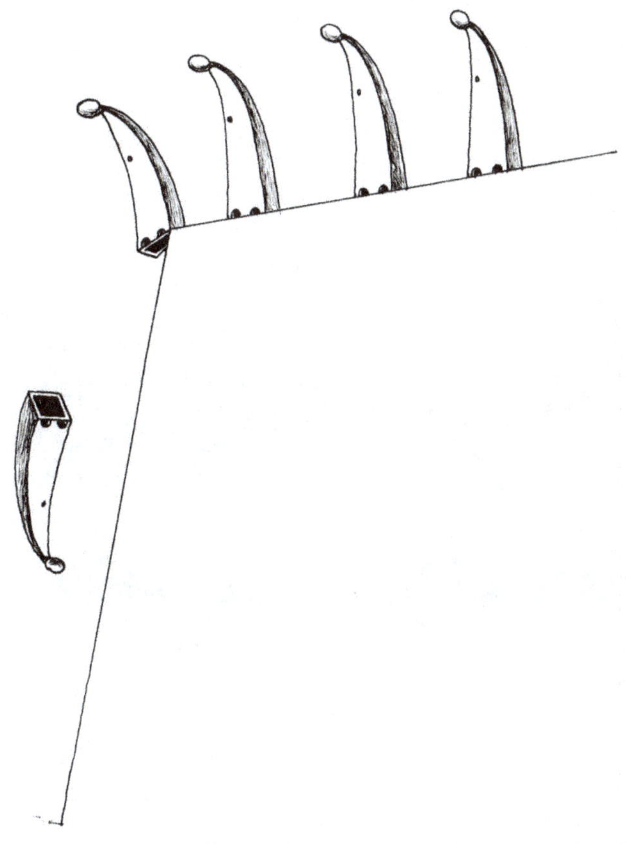

BLIND CONFORMITY

Often time, blind conformity is caused by superior eyesight.

BRAIN

Our brains become meaningless once the total number of people exceeds a certain amount.

BREATHING

When you finally realize that breathing is such a happiness, it is also the moment when the ability to breath is leaving you.

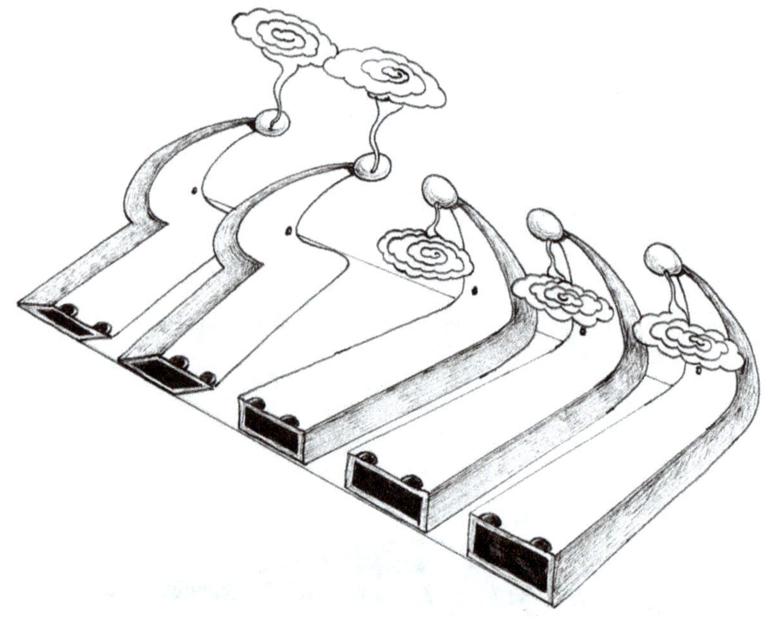

CHATTING

Chatting is a ritual of talking nonsense. Any revelation of truth is impolite during this ritual.

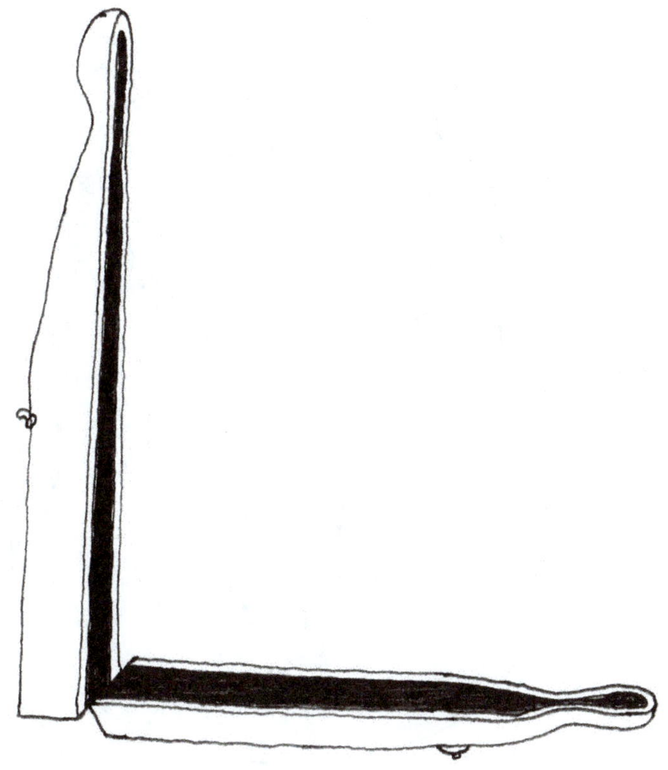

CONCEIT

If women disappear in this world, the reason for rapid human extinction is not that there's nobody to reproduce but that men can never conceit.

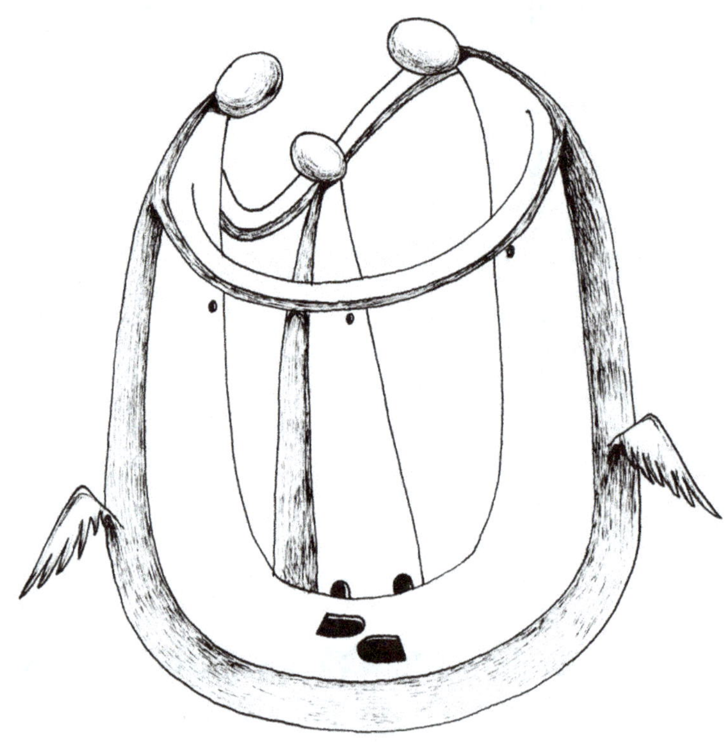

CONJOINED TWINS

Fortune and misfortune are like conjoined twins. You could never live alone with only one of them.

COVERING UP

Covering up something deliberately is similar to revealing it eagerly.

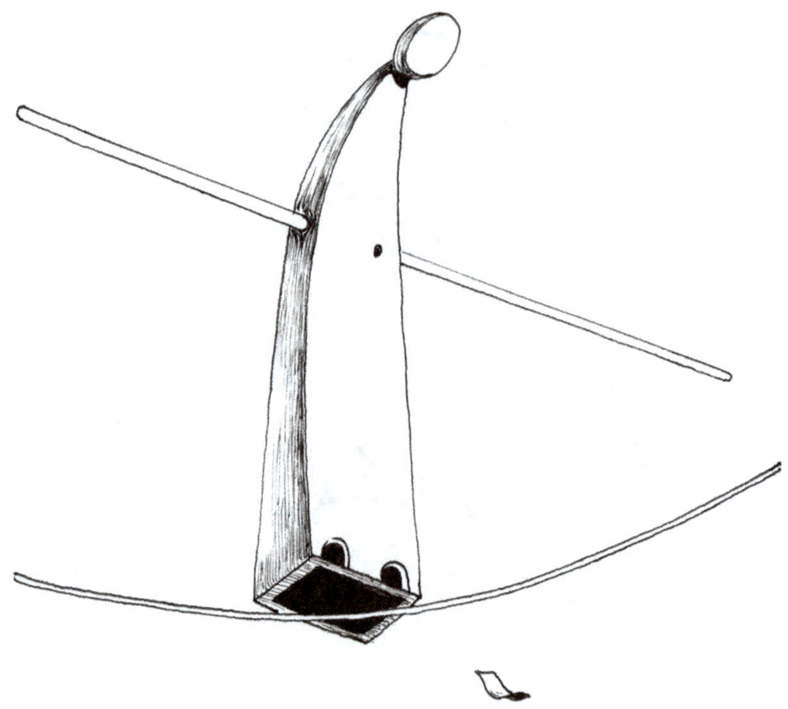

DEATH

Every step you take is going toward death no matter what direction you think you are going.

DEGENERATION

The evolution of spirit will eventually lead to the degeneration of body.

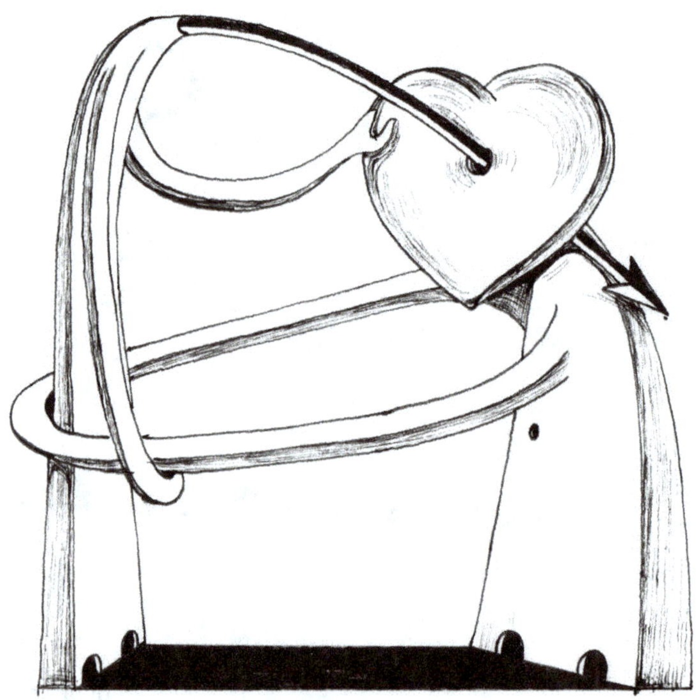

DEPENDENCE

The more you depend on something, the greater chance you will be hurt by it.

DEVELOPMENT

The sole criterion to judge a country's level of development is EDUCATION.

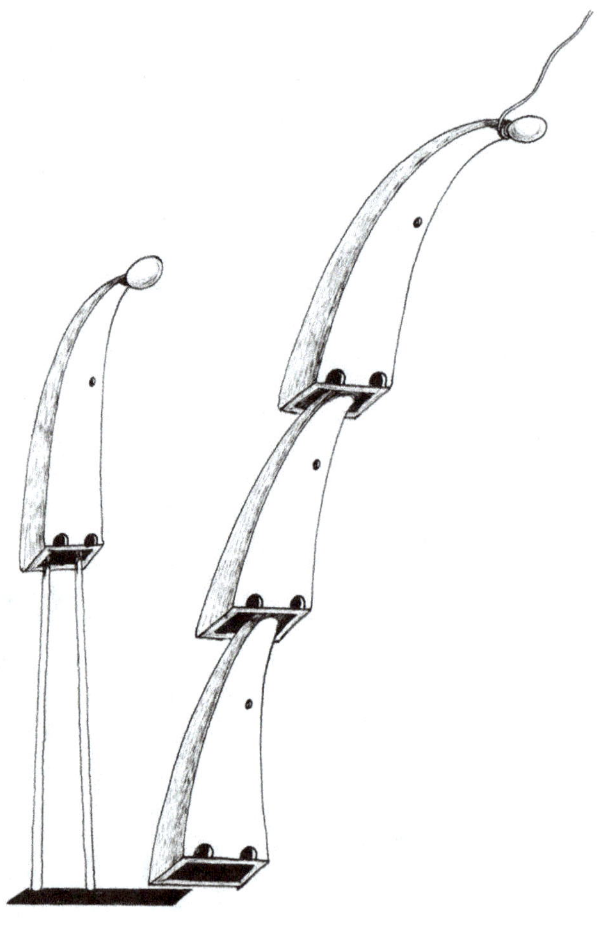

ELEVATING

There are many ways to elevate yourself, but there is only one goal: to fall.

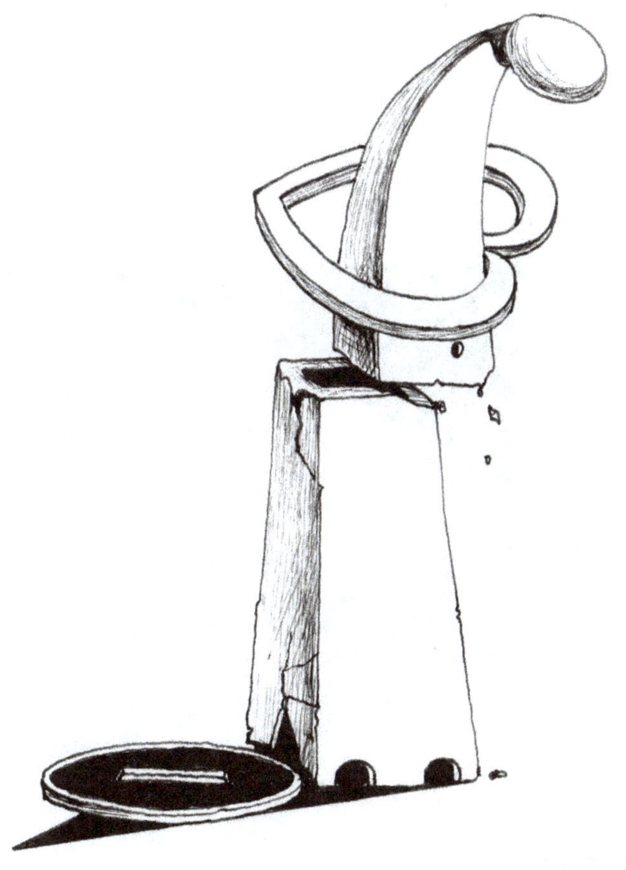

FALLING APART

All the advice we have received will fall apart either at the moment when love comes or when money is lost.

FEAR AND TREMBLE

Sailing safely all the time makes people fear and tremble. Instead, some windy waves would actually make them feel at ease.

FIGHTING

The more incapable of the fighter, the more honorable the fight is.

FLATTERING

Flattering shows a kind of rage. This kind of rage get to explode when a sweet plan deep inside you must be accomplished through an evil figure.

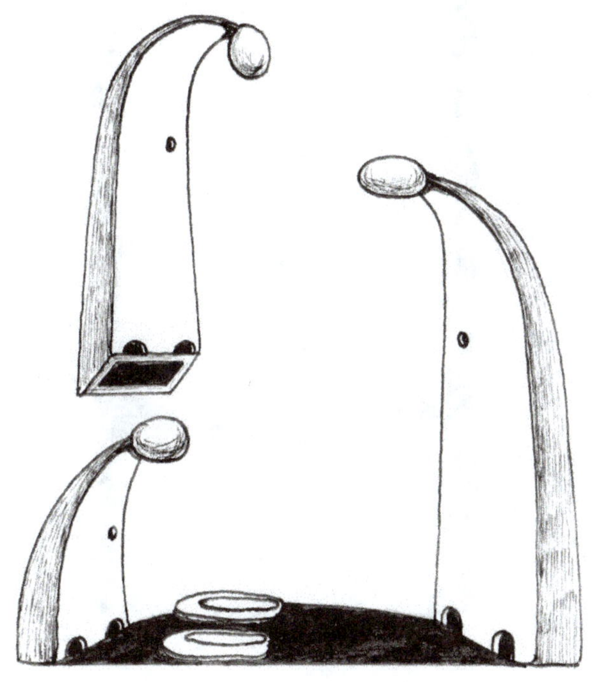

FOOTPRINTS
A man must stop moving to appreciate his footprints.

FOR THE SHOW

Most people live just for a show, even though audiences are all shut outside the door.

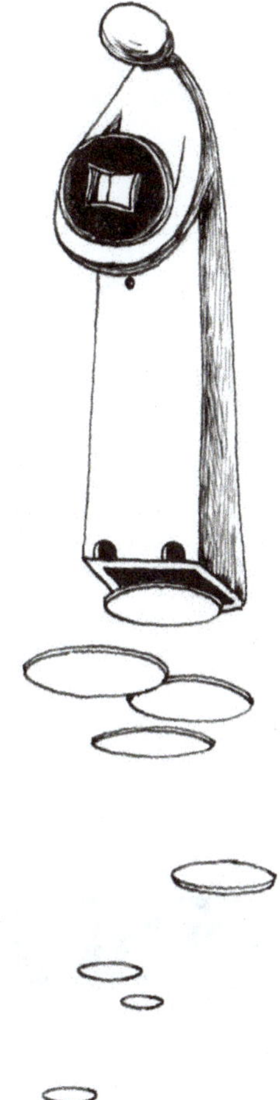

GAIN AND LOSS

It is said that GAINING is when you picked up one dollar. It is also said that LOSING is when you picked up one hundred dollars and then lost ninety-nine dollars.

GETTING A HOUSE

Getting a house; Losing the whole universe.

GO WITH THE TIDE

Going with the tide only works for the fish. People would just sink.

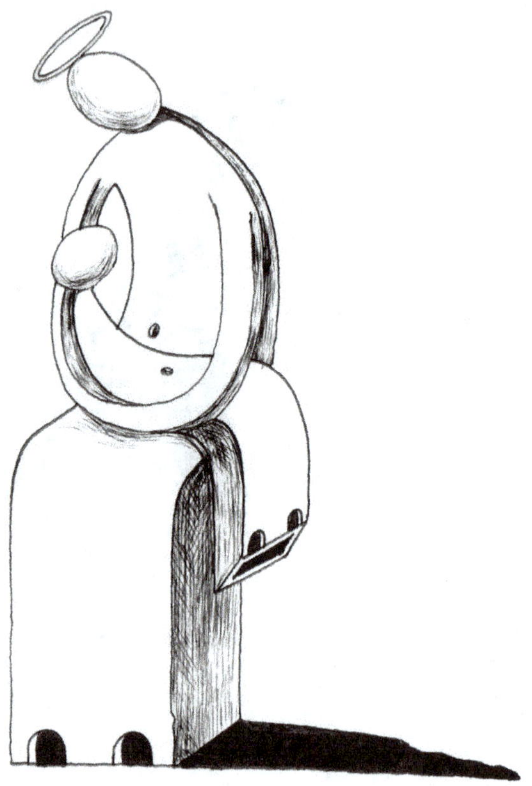

GOD

Everyone's first god is his or her mother.

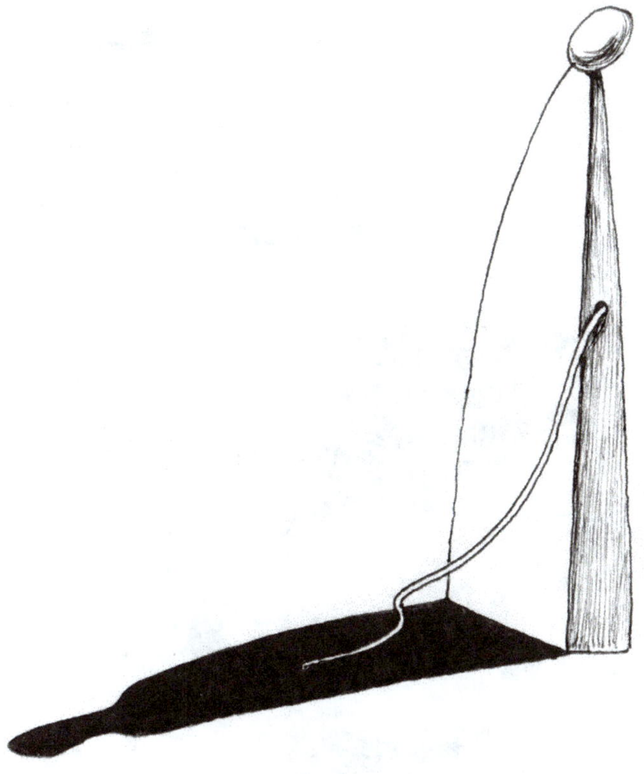

HAVING A TAIL

Only those animals who cannot jump into the air think that having a tail is shameful.

HERITAGE

Money is the most unrespectable heritage.

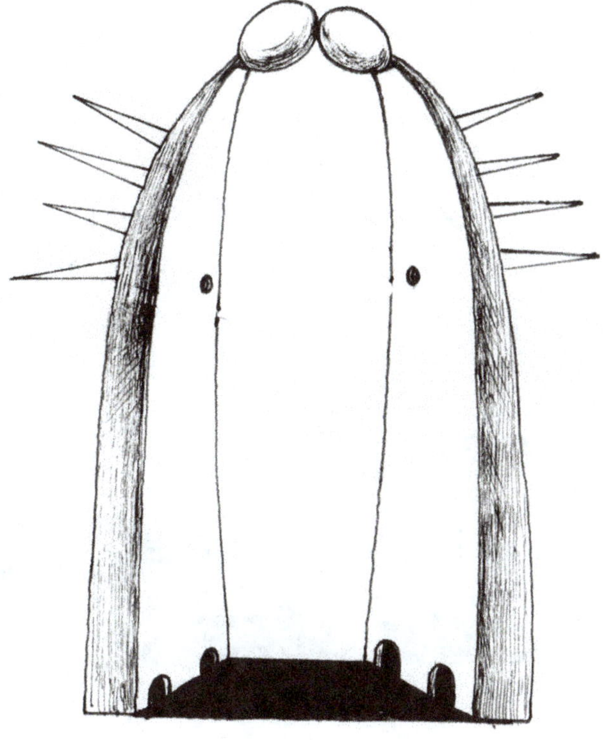

HUMANS

Humans are strange – seeing enemies in disasters but generating compassion at the same time; seeing friends winning lotteries but generating rage at the same time.

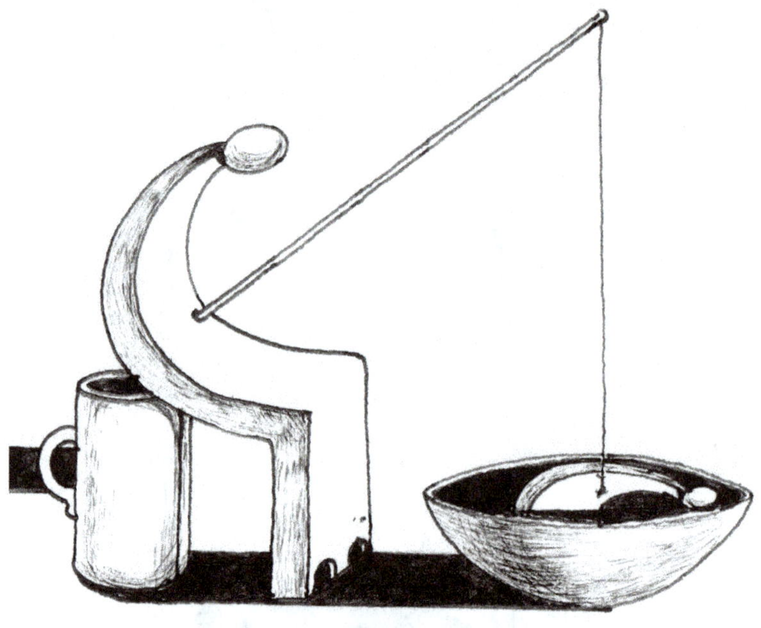

JOY

There are two types of joy. One is based on suffering of human and the other is based on suffering of animals.

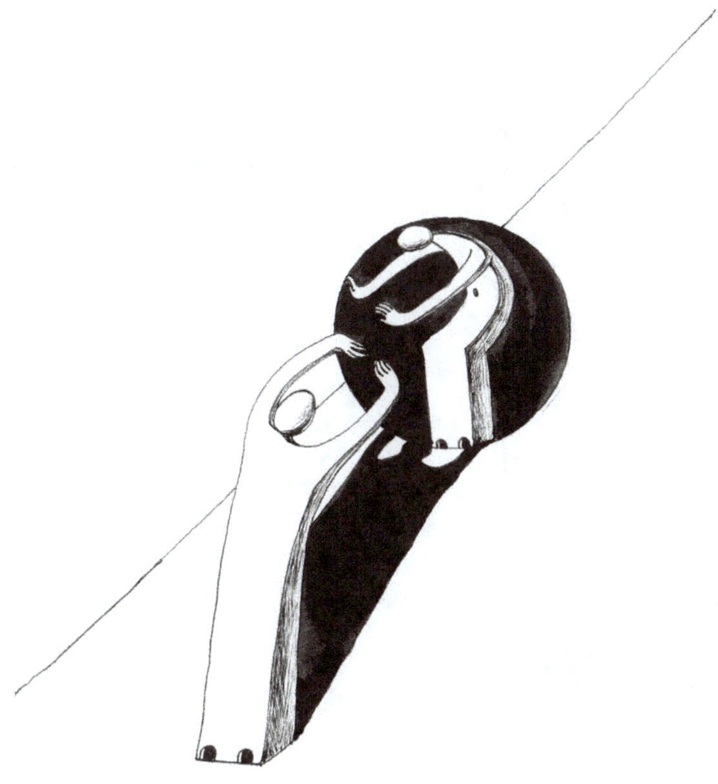

LEISURE TIME

An everlasting leisure for every married woman is to transform her husband. The beauty of this leisure is that she would never succeed but would enjoy it forever.

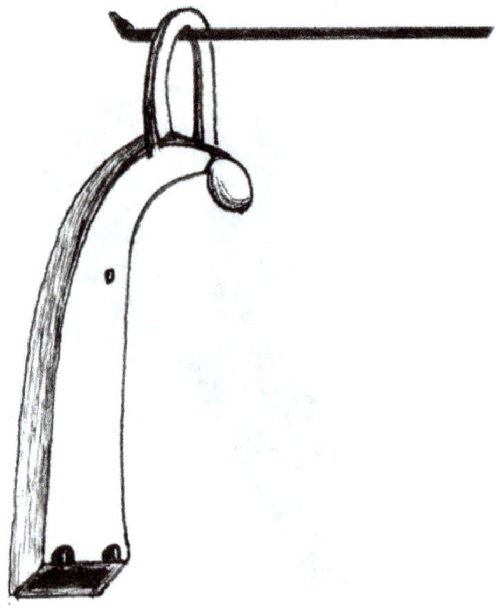

LETTING GO

It is an insider knowledge to people who are hanged in air: man can let go of anything except for the hands.

LUXURY

Leisure time is the most luxurious luxury.

MAKE UP

In this world, money is the only thing whose value can be made up.

MASKING

When a man pursues something elegant, he would mask it with vulgarity. When a woman pursues something vulgar, she would mask it with elegance.

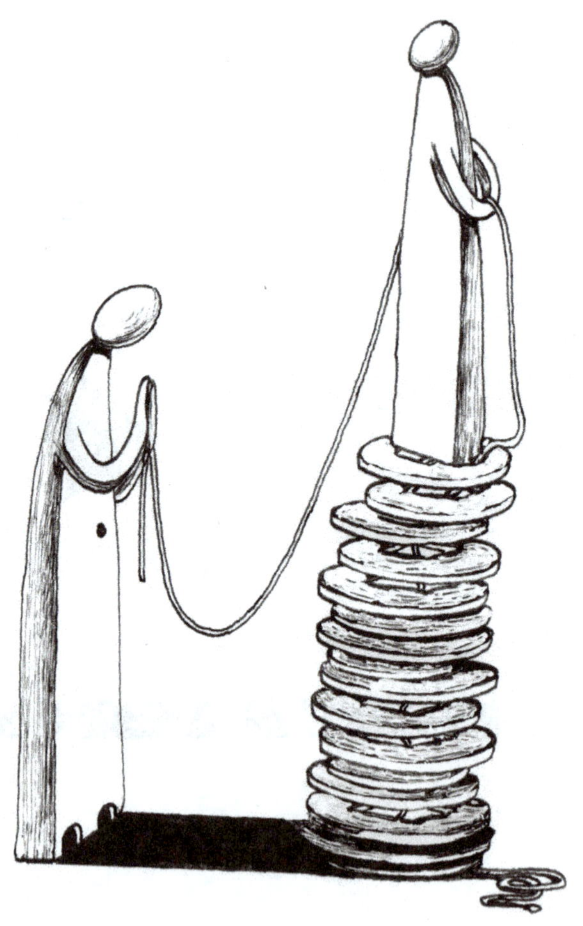

MONEY
Everything that money can bring will also disappear with money.

MOSQUITO NETS

As long as human still need mosquito nets, they are never the wisest of all creatures.

NOBODY WISHES

Nobody wishes to die while they are alive. Nobody wishes to live over again while they are dying.

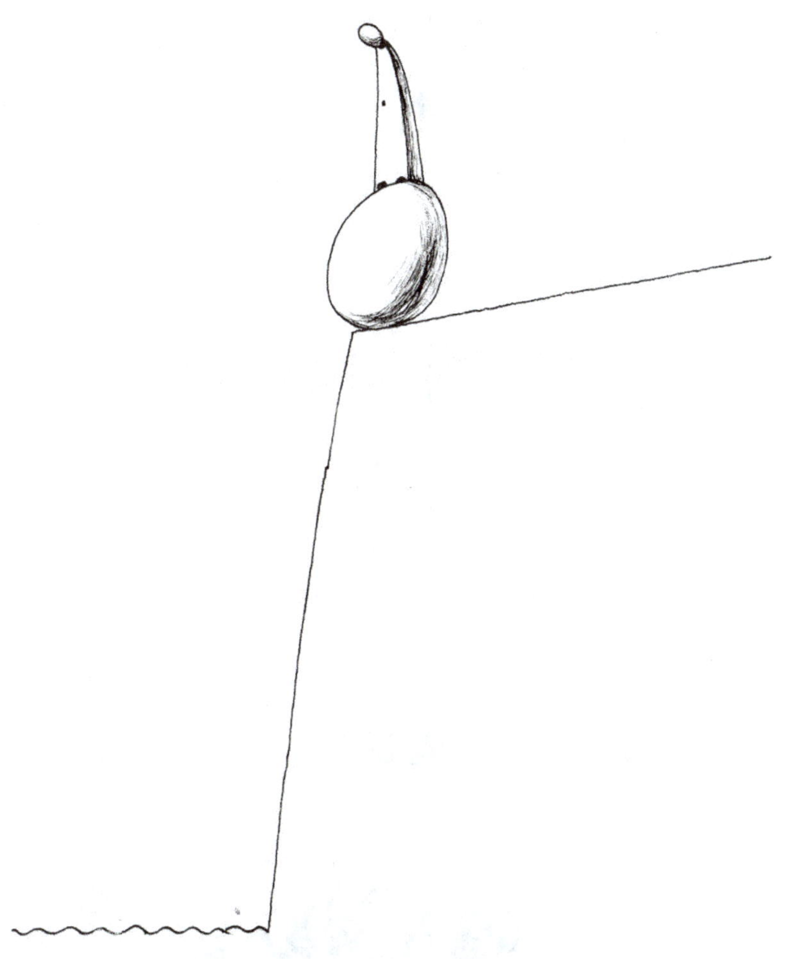

ONE'S MIND

If the ocean can broaden one's mind, why do people always jump into it? Therefore, a broad mind needs the same amount of training just like for building muscle. A simple observation of nature is worthless.

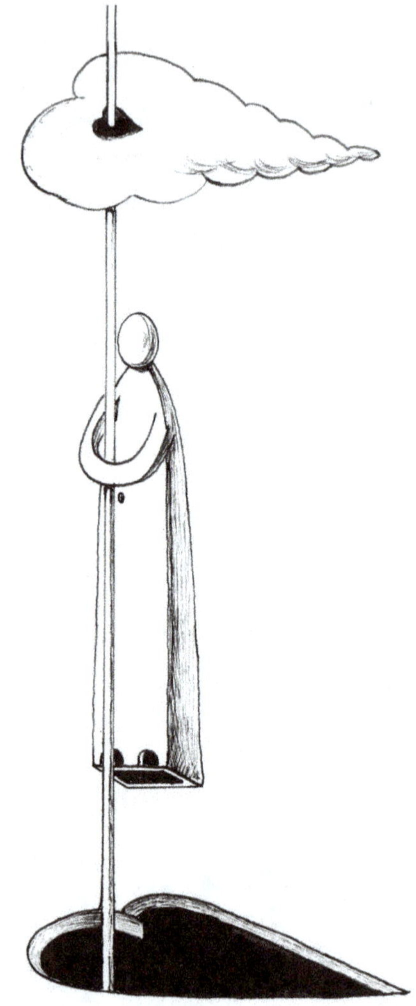

OWING

A man must get aids from the world if he has something to love. Thus, a man must also owe the world.

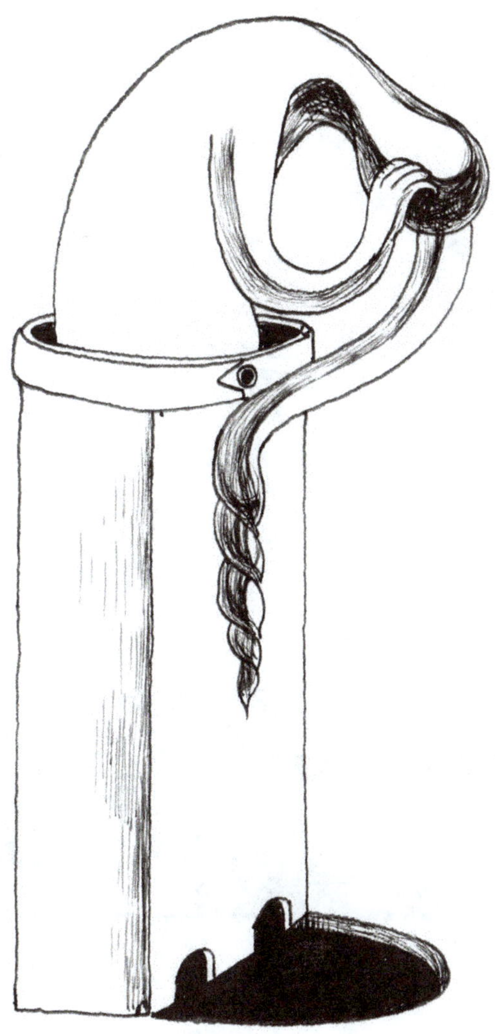

PANTS

The major function of pants is to hide our shy legs as we take the wrong path.

PAY OFF

Waiting for payback is a greater pay off than pay off itself.

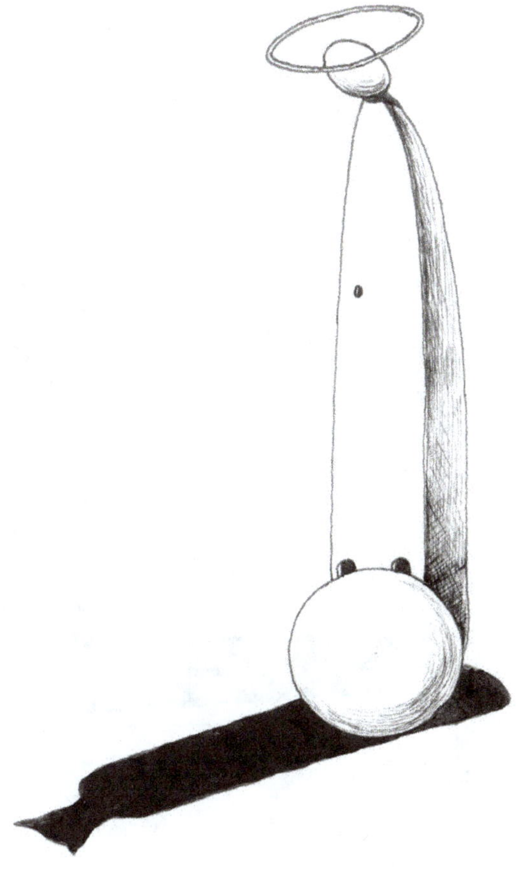

PICKING UP

You should first empty your hands when you want to pick up something.

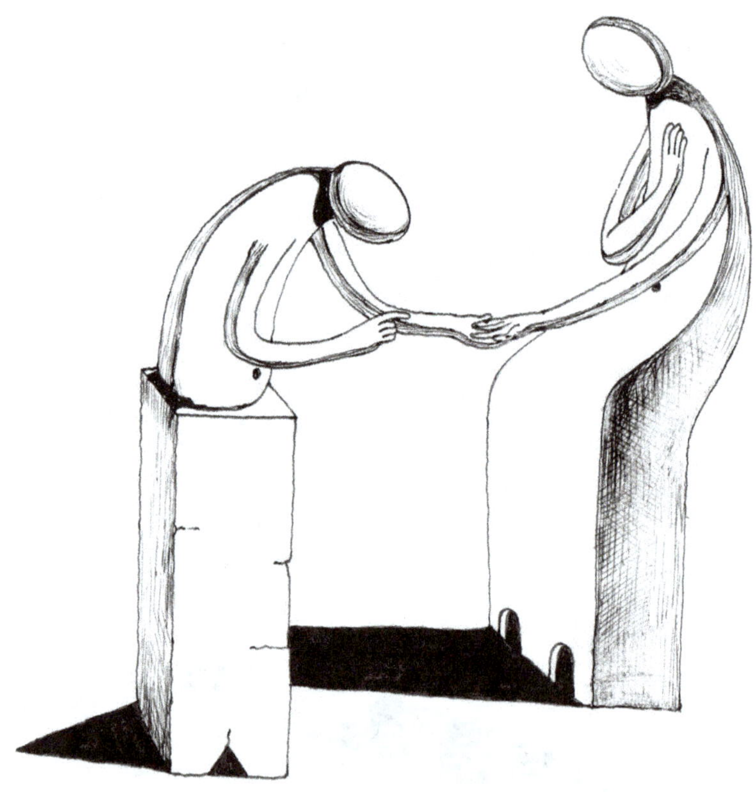

PLEASANT TO THE EARS

There are only two kinds of people whose words are pleasant to the ears: someone with elegant gestures or a despicable purpose.

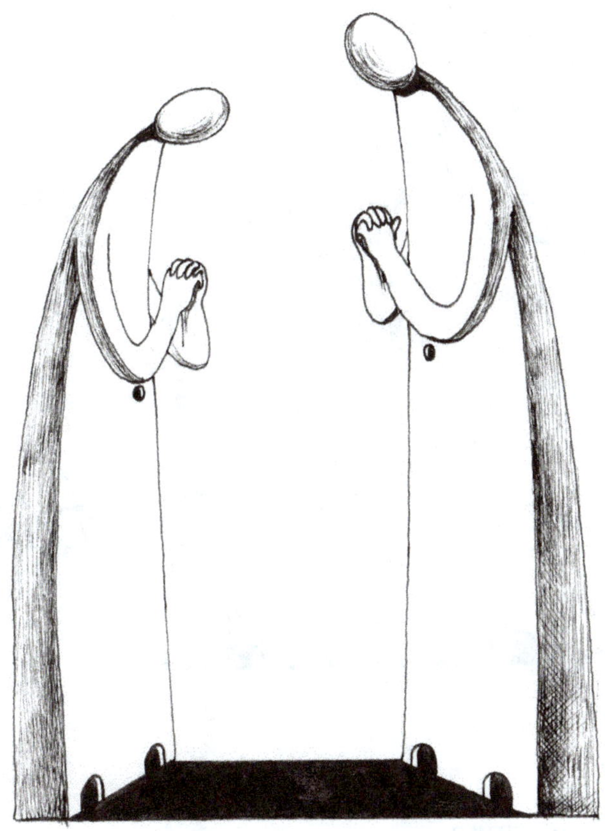

POLITENESS

Politeness has a stern power. It can also show defiance to others beside showing respect.

PRAISING EACH OTHER

We despise people who praise themselves but advocate everybody to praise each other. This only worsens the social atmosphere.

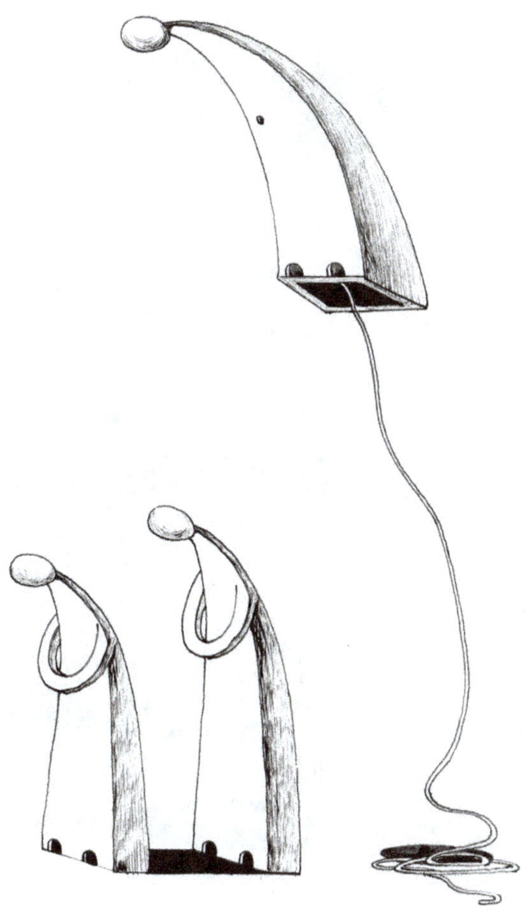

PRIDE

The worst moment of life is showing pride in absence of a witness.

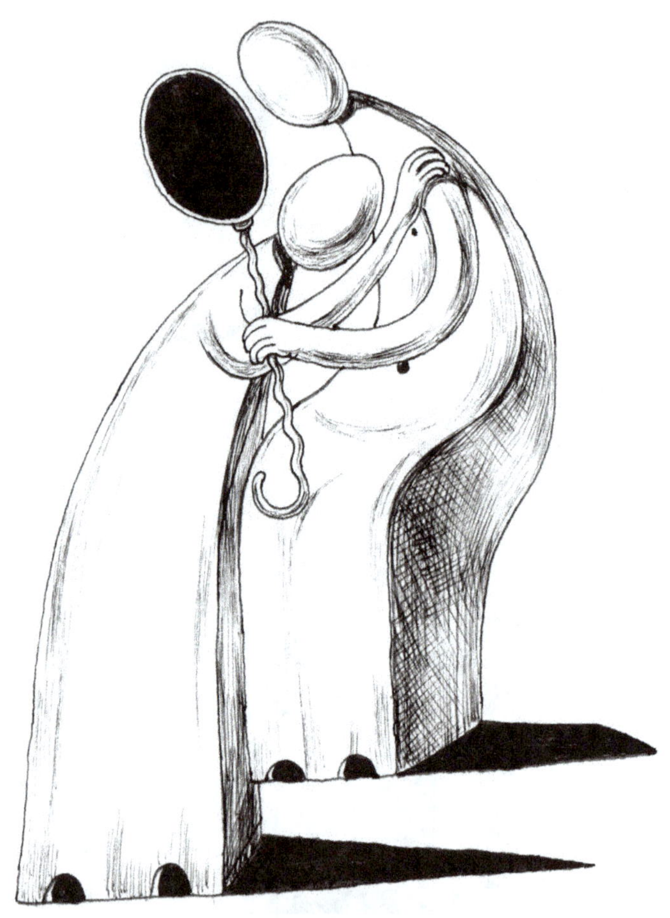

PUBERTY AND BREAST-FEEDING PERIOD

Women are always in puberty whereas men are always in breastfeeding period.

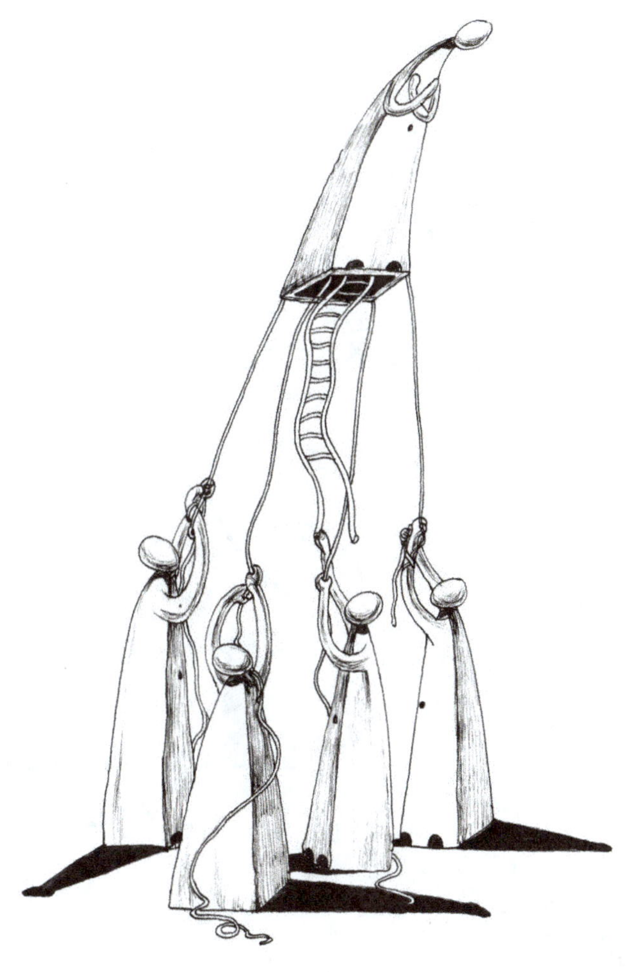

PUFFING

Puffing is a kind of poetic murder.

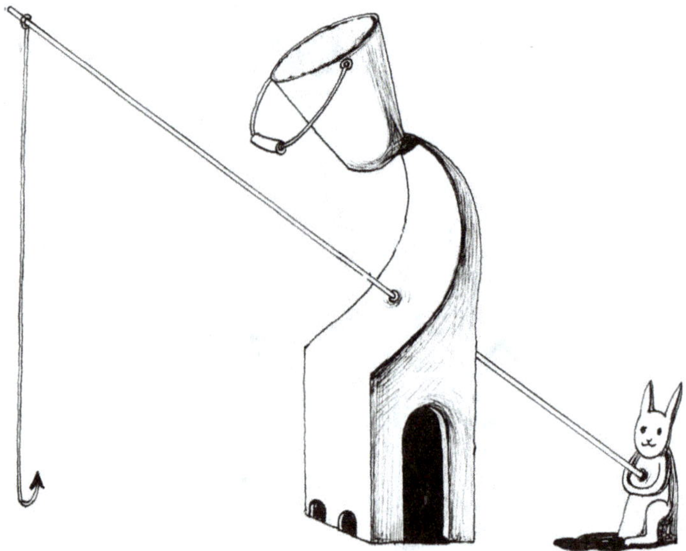

RECEIVING

We often receive nothing on the thing that we put in sustained efforts but receive unexpected gains on another thing that we may not even pay attention to. However, if we did not make that efforts in the first place, we will end up with neither of them.

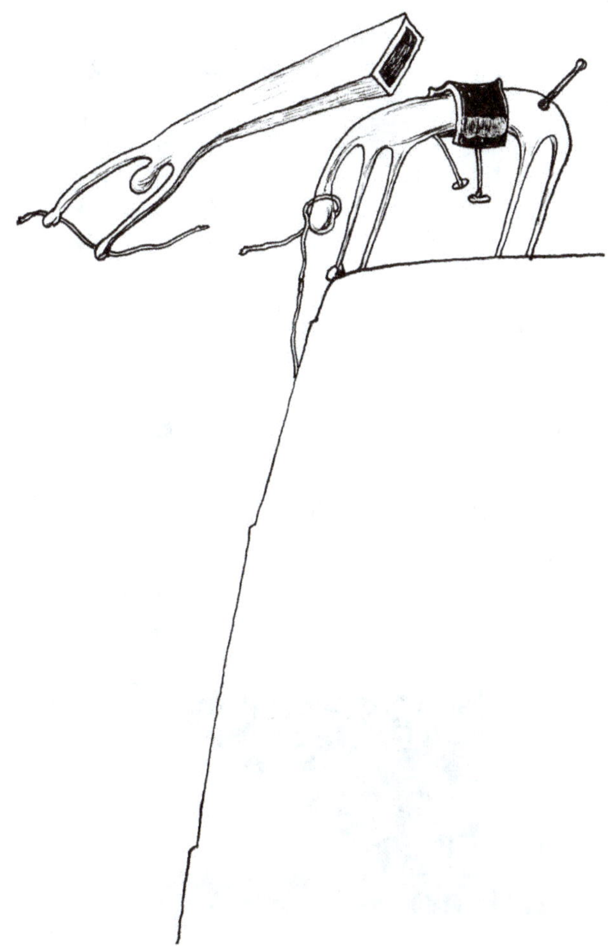

REINING THE HORSE NEAR THE CLIFF

The attempt to rein a horse near the edge of a cliff is for saving the horse. However, the horse rider will continue to move forward due to inertia.

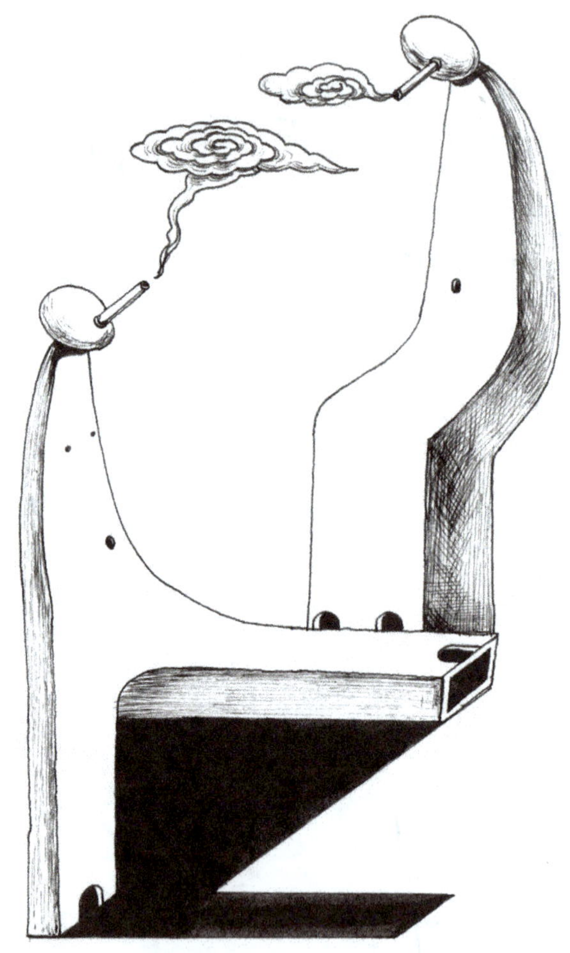

RUDENESS

Women should not imitate the rudeness of men in order to cater him, because even the rudest man still wishes for a sweet woman.

SALVES

Human beings are not their own masters but are rather slaves of their own desires.

SCHOOL

Suffering is a real school. Only the graduates of this school are truely strong.

SECRET

If you want a secret to go into public, the best way is to ask someone to keep it.

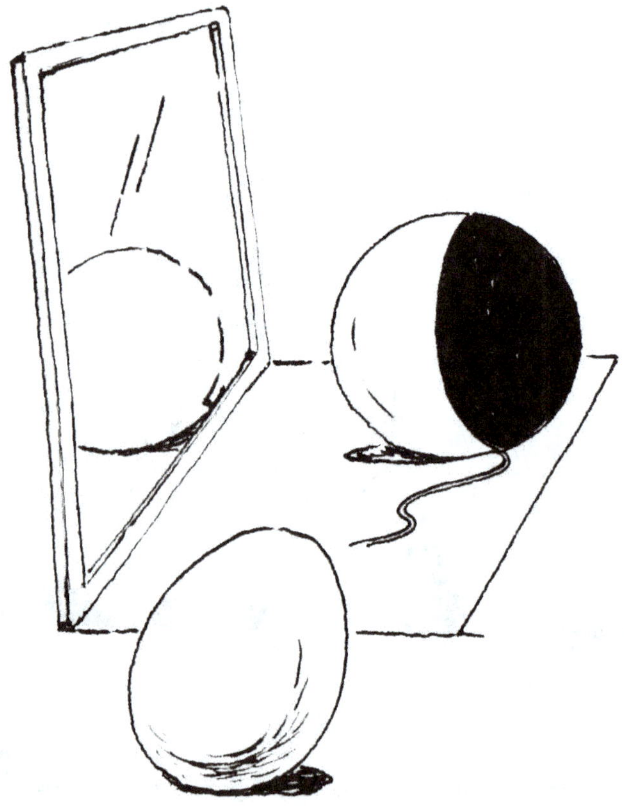

SEEING OTHERS

Anyone would become a wise man if he sees himself as clear as he sees others.

SELF

It is impossible to understand yourself just as it is impossible to feel itching when you do it to yourself.

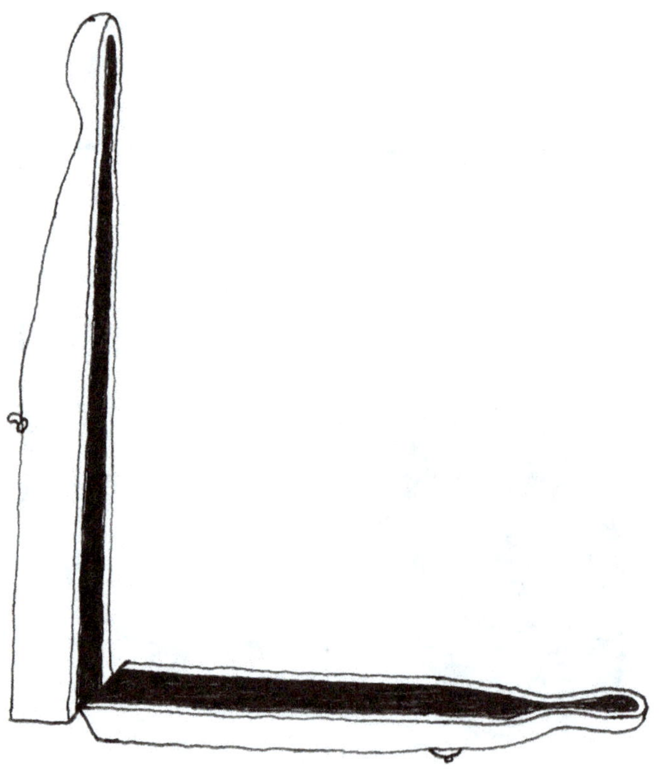

SHOWING OFF

If women disappear in this world, the reason of the rapidly vanishing population is not because of no one is bearing children but the men can never show off their ability anymore.

SPEAKING

The guiltier people feel inside, the louder they speak. Speaking at a low key is often more aggressive.

STRUGGLING

Life is a process of people initially struggling to get out of others' control but eventually giving up.

SWEETNESS

Sweetness is an illusion that occurs when two people feel like they belong to each other. It will disappear as soon as when the feeling is confirmed.

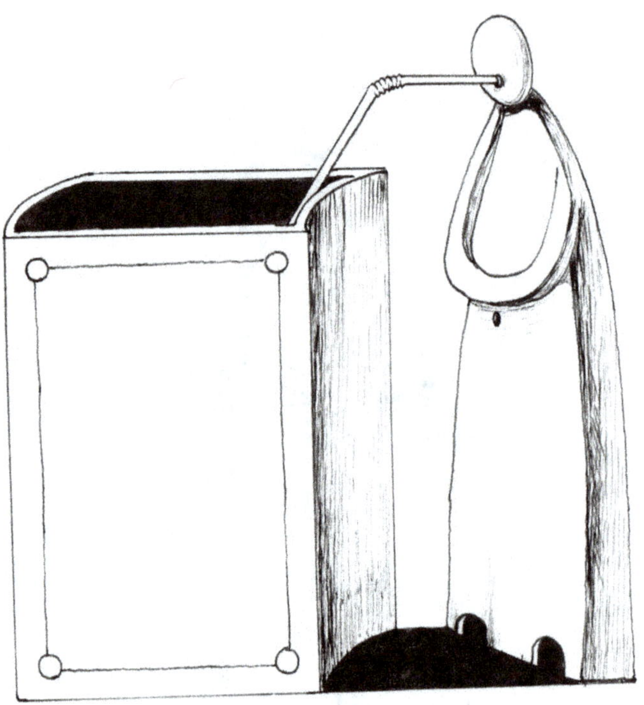

TEXTBOOKS

The key to education is not to supply children with textbooks but the contents in them.

THE ANIMALS

Animals are rarely interested in inedible stuffs, which predestinated them to be happier than humans.

THE AUTHOR

To create a piece of work and to give birth to a child are the most miraculous thing on earth. At some point, the author is equivalent to God.

THE BEAUTIFUL THING

Sunshine is not really a beautiful thing for snow.

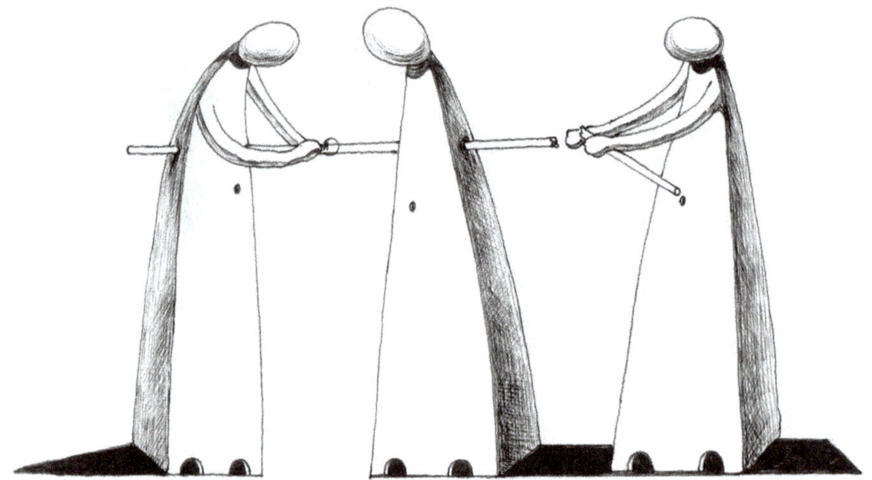

THE BOTHERING

The greatest bothering in life is that everyone who loves you tries to change you.

THE CONSOLATION

For people who are trapped down in mud and unable to pull themselves up, their last consolation is to see others trapped down there too.

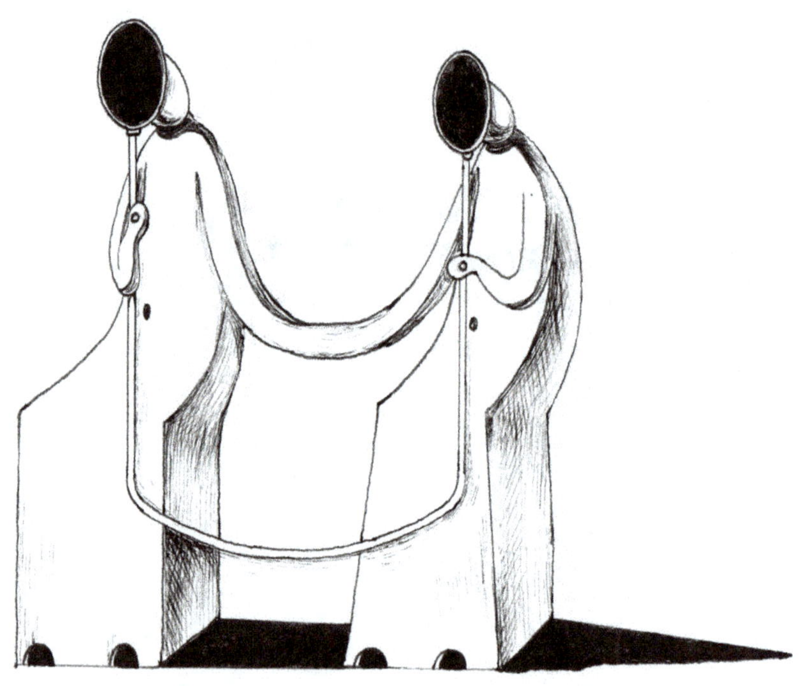

THE CONVERSATION

Only eye contact can be called CONVERSATION. We are actually in silence when we talk through mouths.

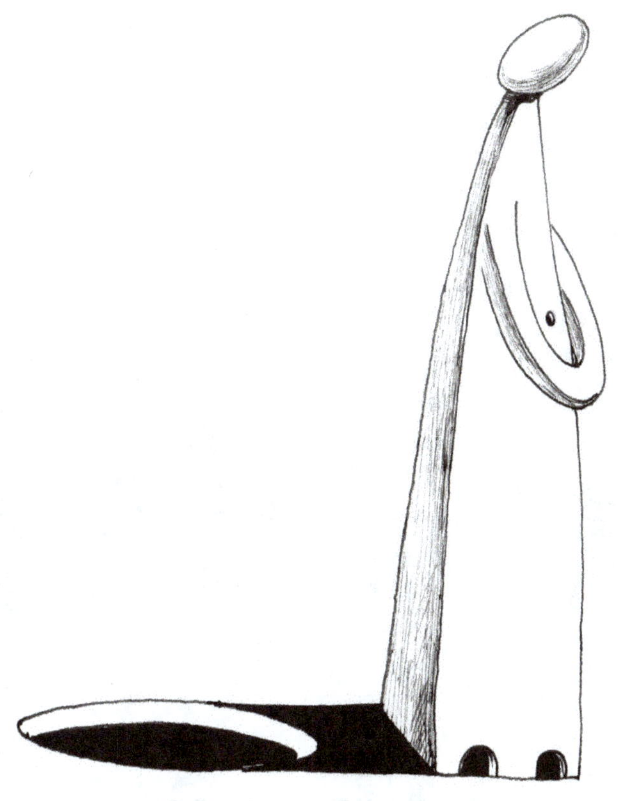

THE COURAGE

Occasionally, more courage are needed to step back than to attack.

THE CROWD

There is always a force that makes us fear of being alone but feeling relieved with a crowd.

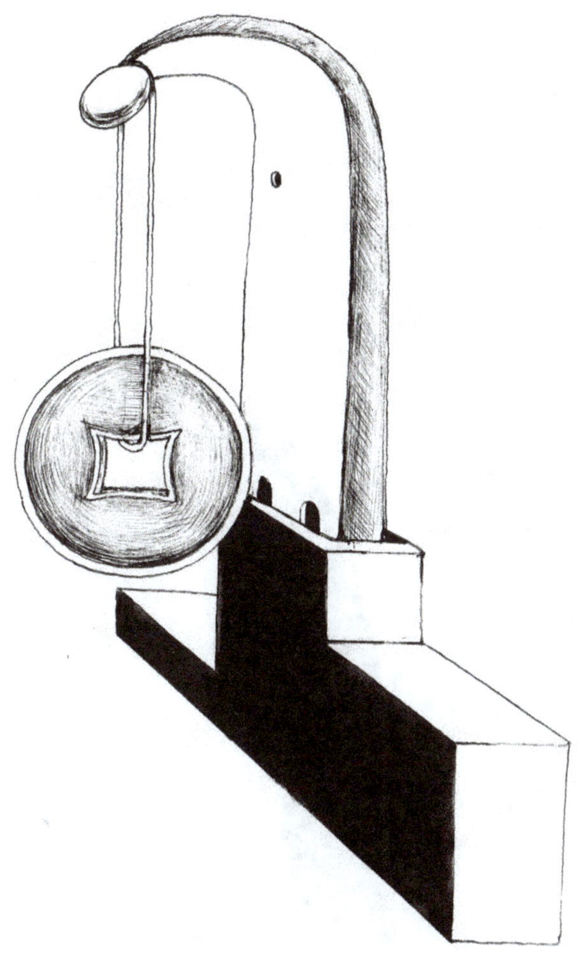

THE CURSE

The reason that human beings are away from happiness is because that they thought fortune is a blessing rather than a curse.

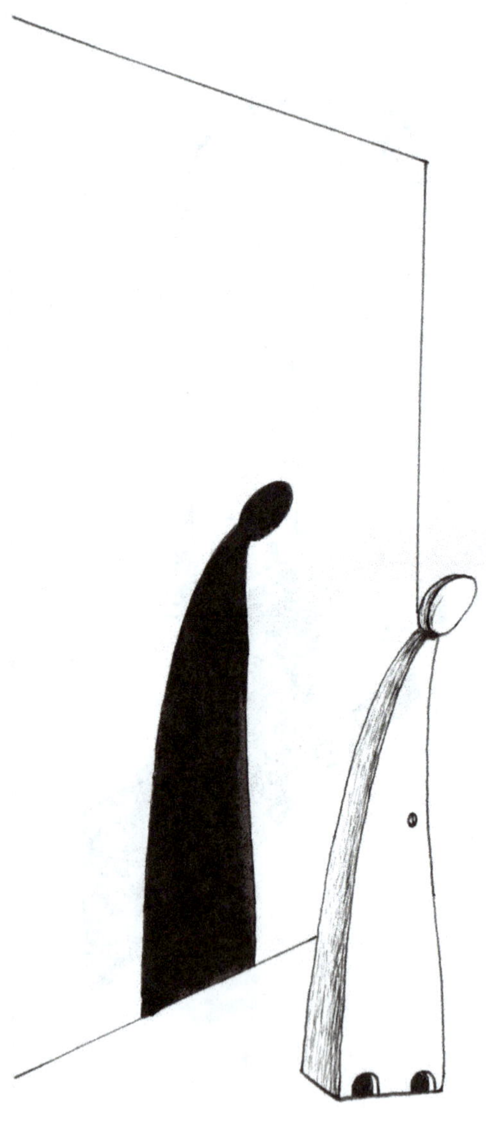

THE DARKNESS

Do not be afraid to step into darkness if you want to walk under the light.

THE DEBATE

Debate is a kind of duel. Winning is skill-based instead of truth-based.

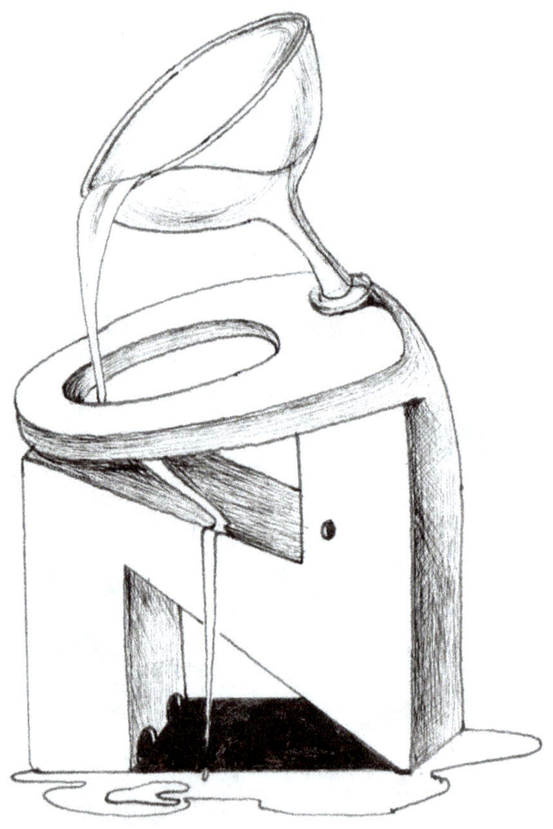

THE DESPAIR

People who have no treasures in their hearts love to treat their despair with extravagance and waste.

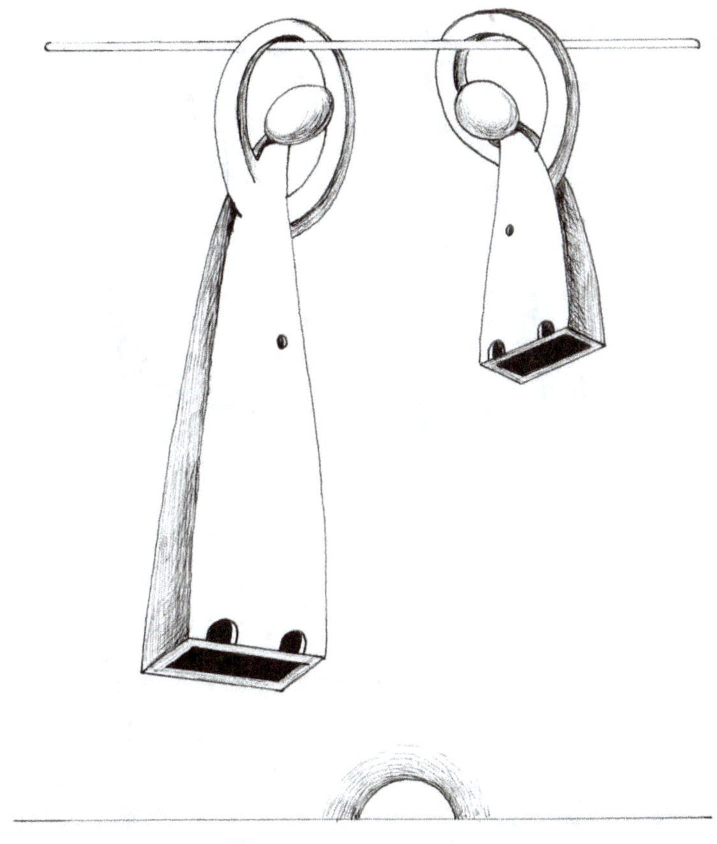

THE DIFFERENCE

The difference between children and adults is that adults are a bit taller than children.

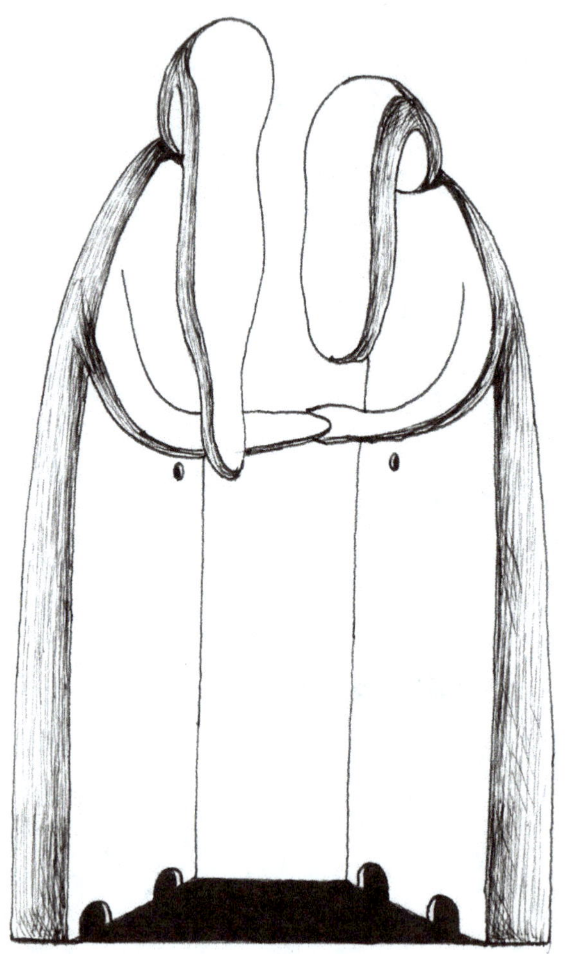

THE DRESS FOR THE FACE

There will eventually be a day when human beings create outfits for their faces. In fact, it is the most embarrassing part of the body.

THE EXPECTATIONS

People are greater than saints when they expect nothing, but people are weaker than insects when they expect something.

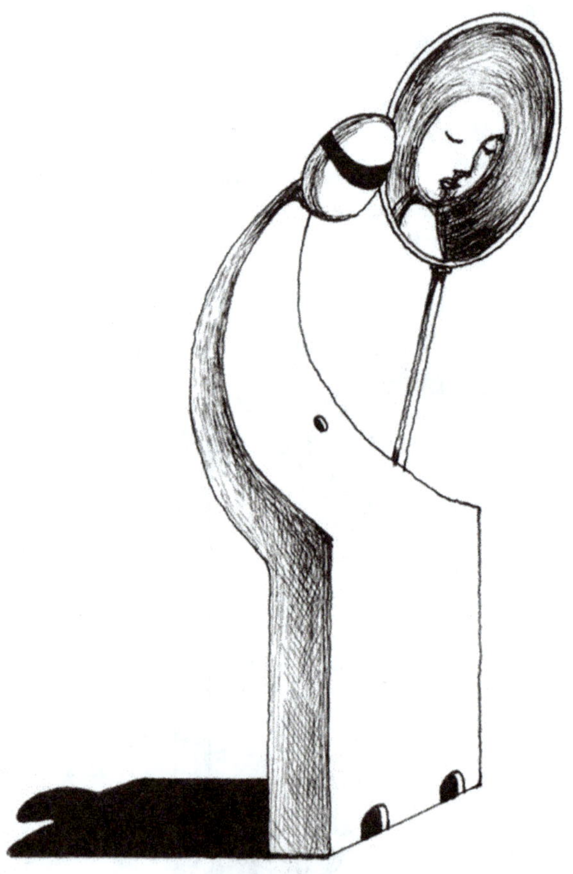

THE FACE

From the early history to the present, no one has REALLY seen the face of oneself.

THE FLOWERS OF HAPPINESS

The flowers of happiness always bloom in the places where we don't even pay attention to.

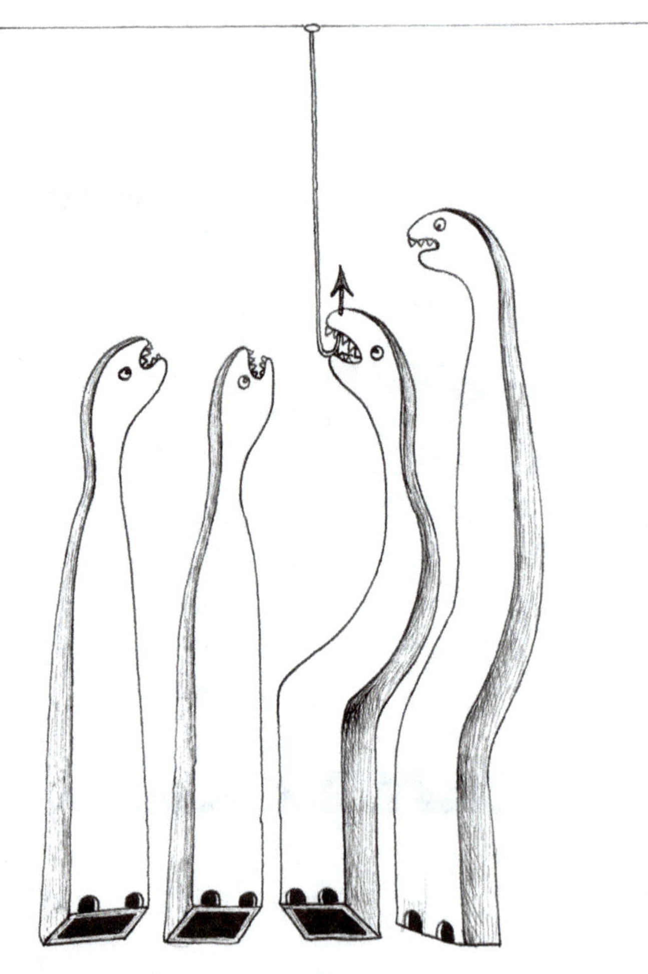

THE FOOD

Fish become food from chasing food on the fishhook.

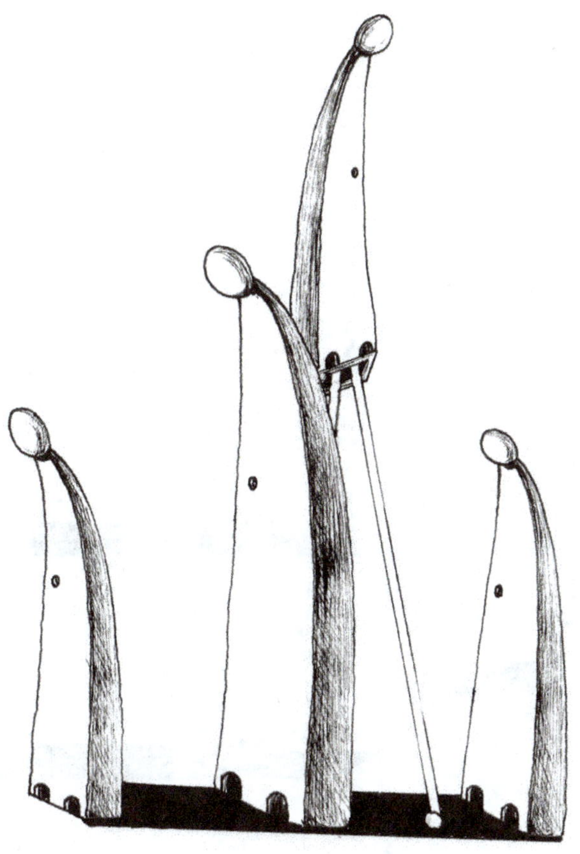

THE FOOTPRINTS

There is an illusion that everyone likes to take a shortcut. In fact, people like to follow other's footprints.

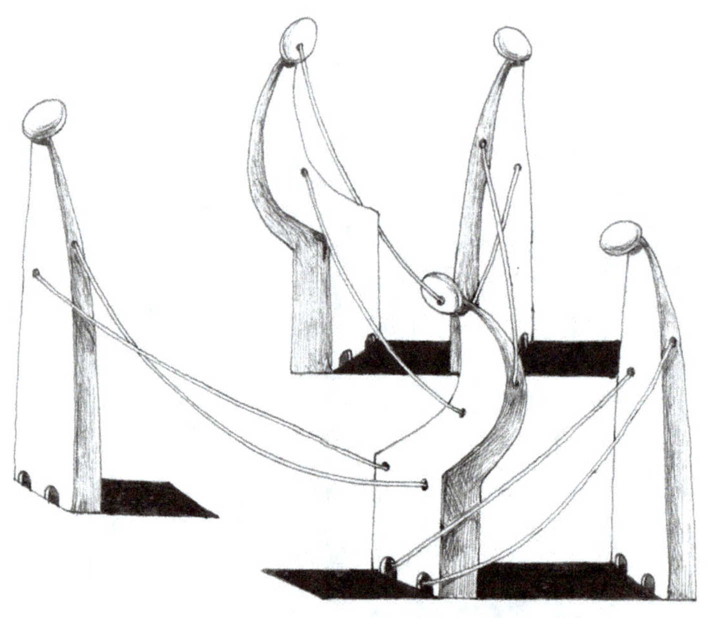

THE FREEDOM

The true freedom is when everyone is equally restricted.

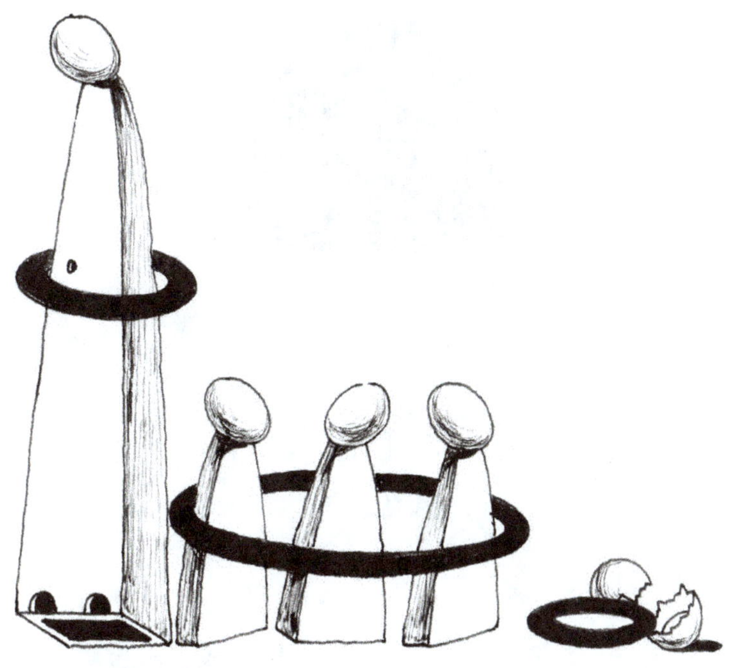

THE FRIENDS

Everyone likes to make friends with people who have similar IQ as themselves. Those who are over or less intelligent are usually hard to find friends.

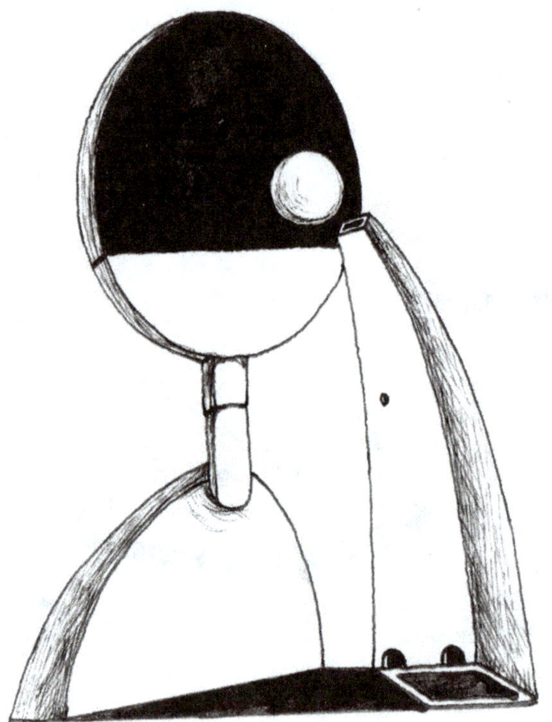

THE FRIENDSHIP

The authentic friendship follows such model: You are annoyed for being together but start to miss each other in separation.

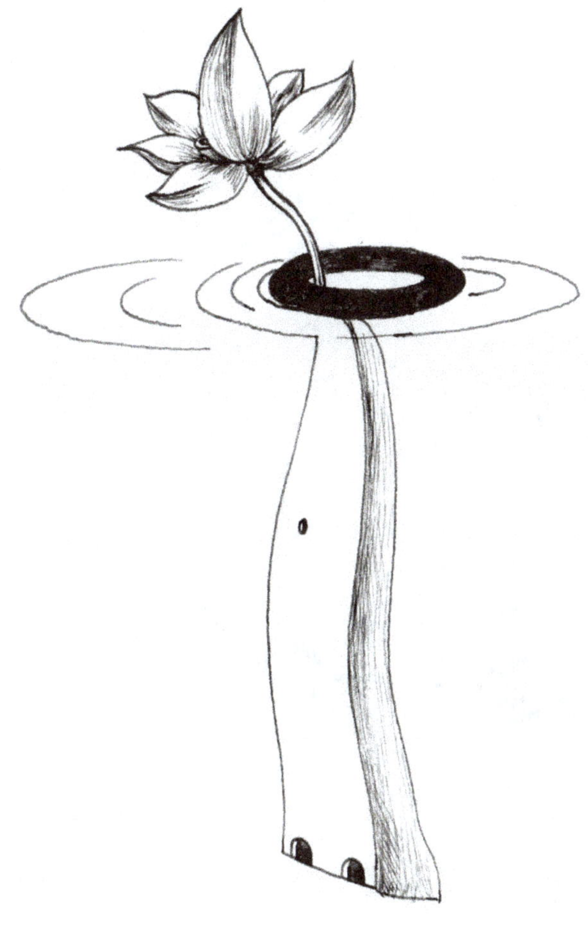

THE GAME

We are all playing a lifelong game of sinking into pains to chase happiness.

THE GENIUSES

It is unfair to label some people as mediocrities, because they show an equally extraordinary talent when persecuting the geniuses.

THE GLORY

Someday we will comfort ourselves that it is a glory to be abused by destiny.

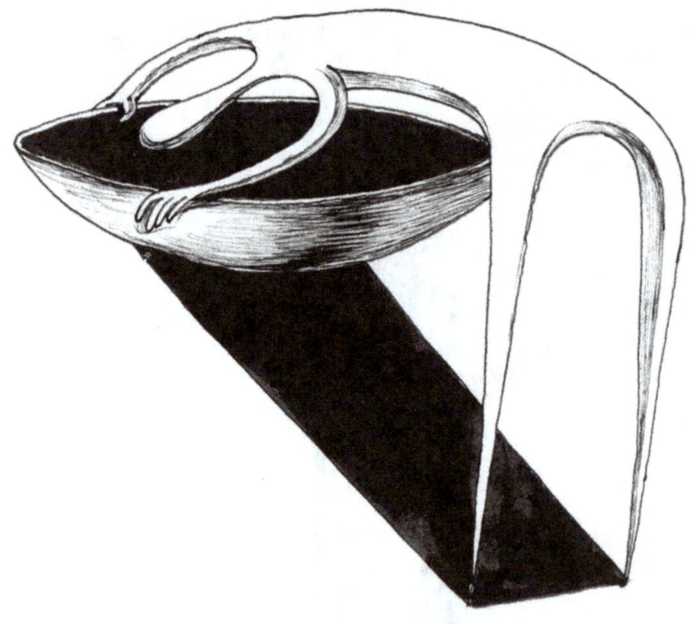

THE GOURMET

If a kind of food can make you full, then it is probably not a gourmet.

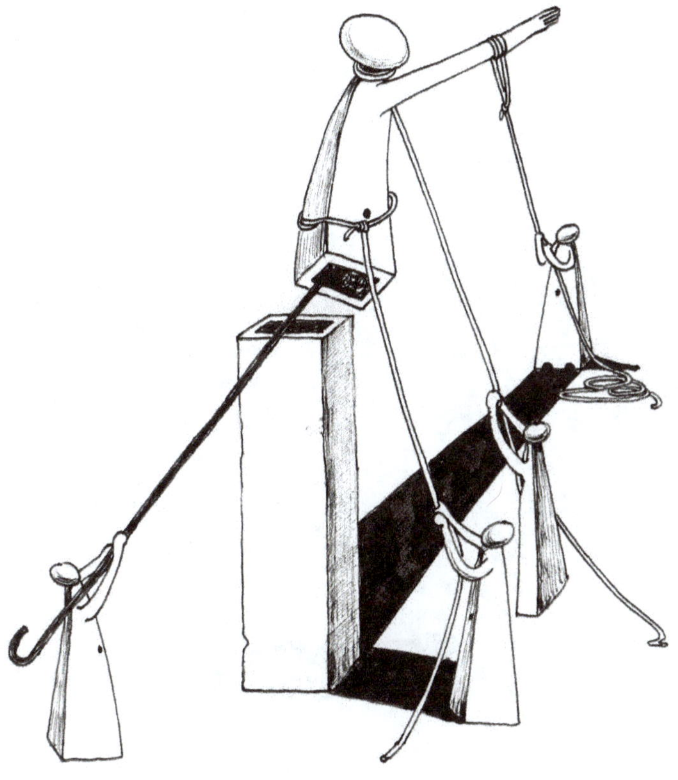

THE GREATNESS

We will never understand how great standing is until the moment we die.

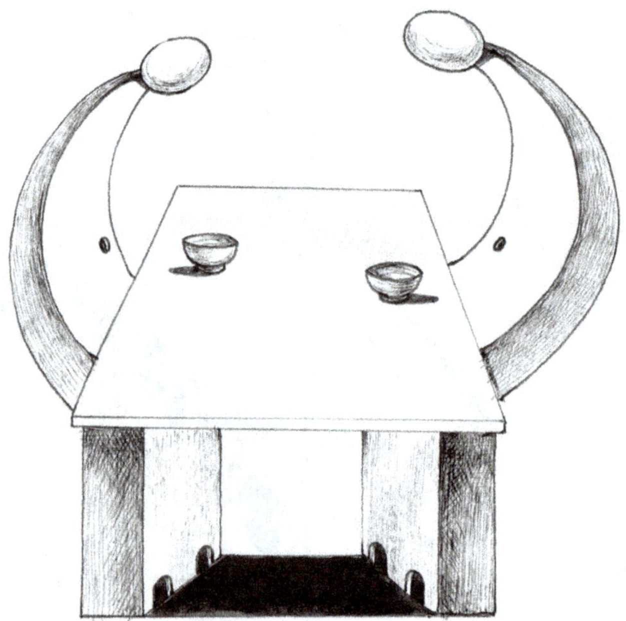

THE HAPPINESS

The less passion in your life, the more likely that you are in happiness.

THE HOSPITAL

Marriage is the best hospital for a psychotic disorder named FALL IN LOVE.

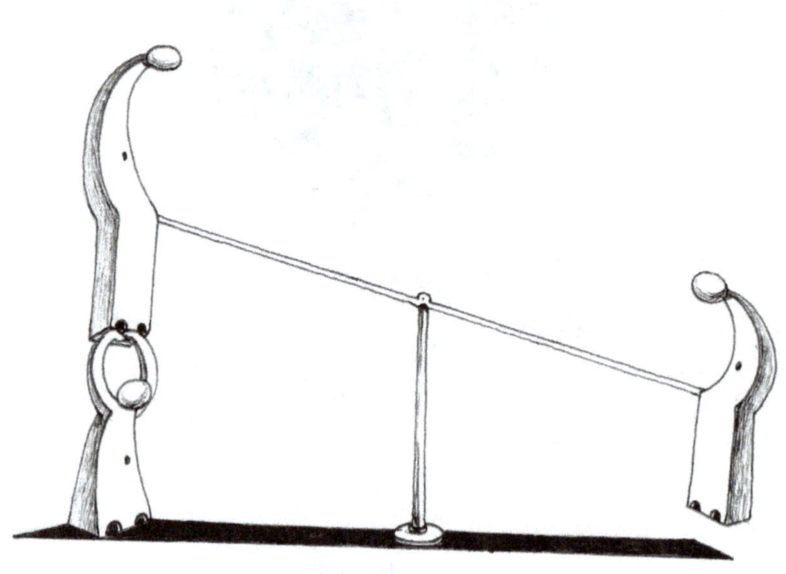

THE JUSTICE

Justice is unseen when comparing only two things. It is seen when all things are put together.

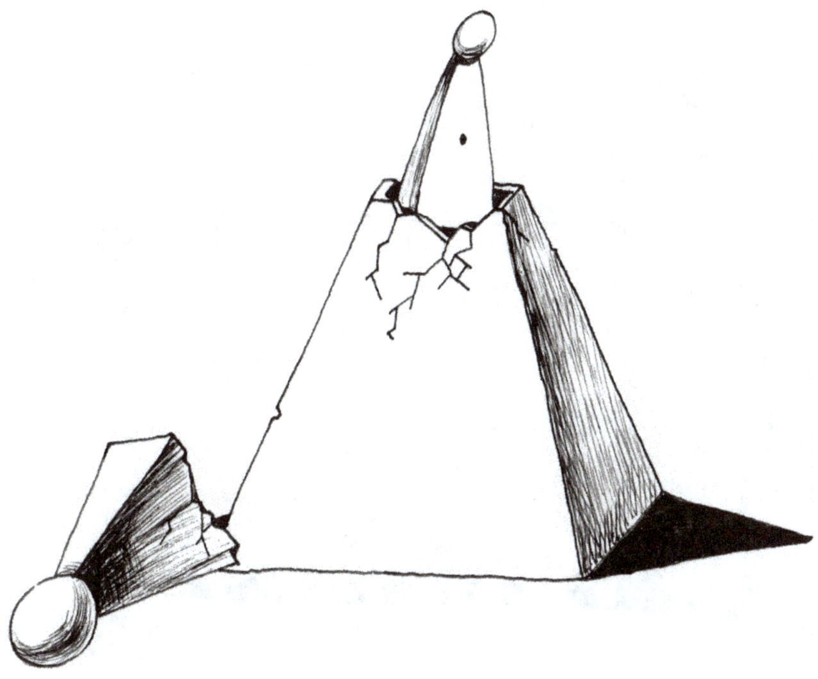

THE KINGDOM

Every kingdom was established by a great man and destroyed by a nobody.

THE KISS

A woman never forgets the men who have kissed her.
A man never forgets the women that he has not yet kissed.

THE LESSONS

It is true that historical lessons help us to seize the current. Ironically, history teaches us that none of the historical events were recorded based on what truly happened.

THE LORD OF CREATIONS

In fact, cats are creators of all rather than humans. Humans are only the brave bodyguards who fight against nature in order to ensure a good night sleep for cats. Humans can get this job because in cats' views humans are the only species that is stupid enough.

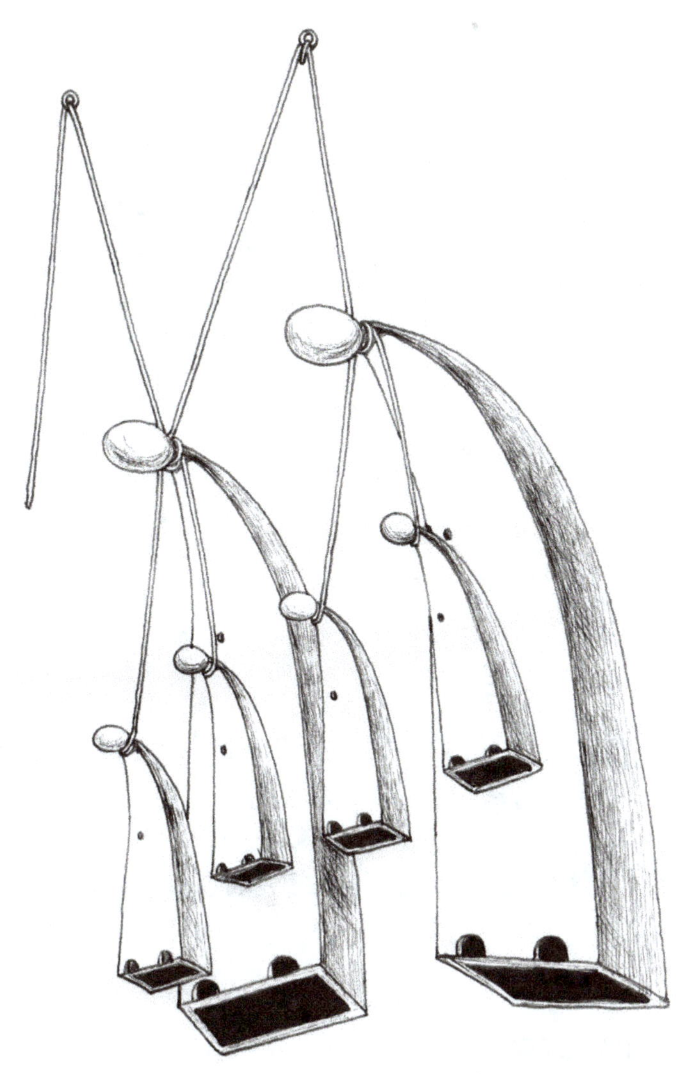

THE NECK

Women love necklace; men love tie. Everyone wants something around the neck.

THE NONSENSES

A child's question leads to your sudden realization: during your years of speaking nonsenses, people were even tired to cut you off.

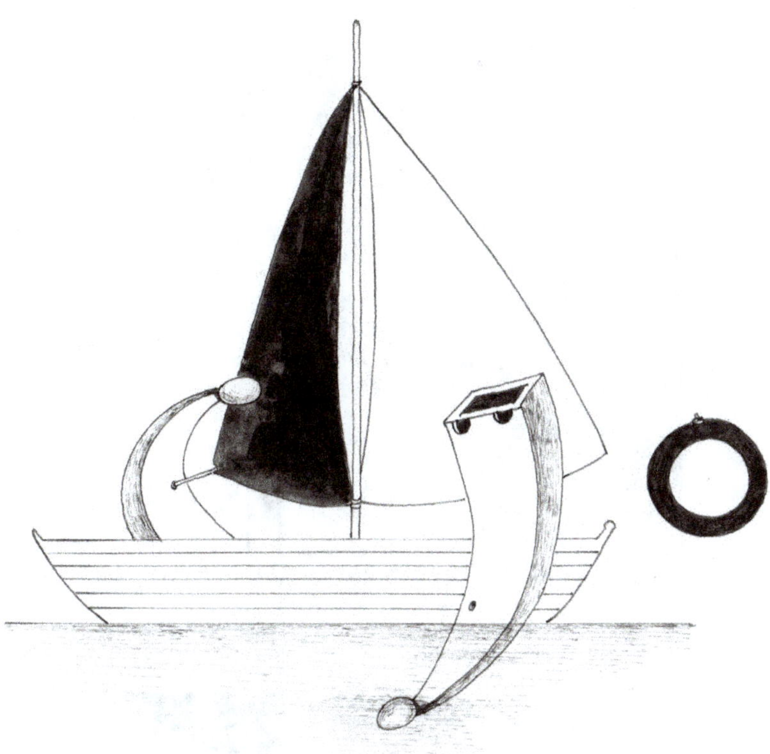

THE OCEAN OF KNOWLEDGE

The ocean of knowledge can help you to reach the shore of dreams, but it can drown you. It depends on if you are sailing above it or falling into it.

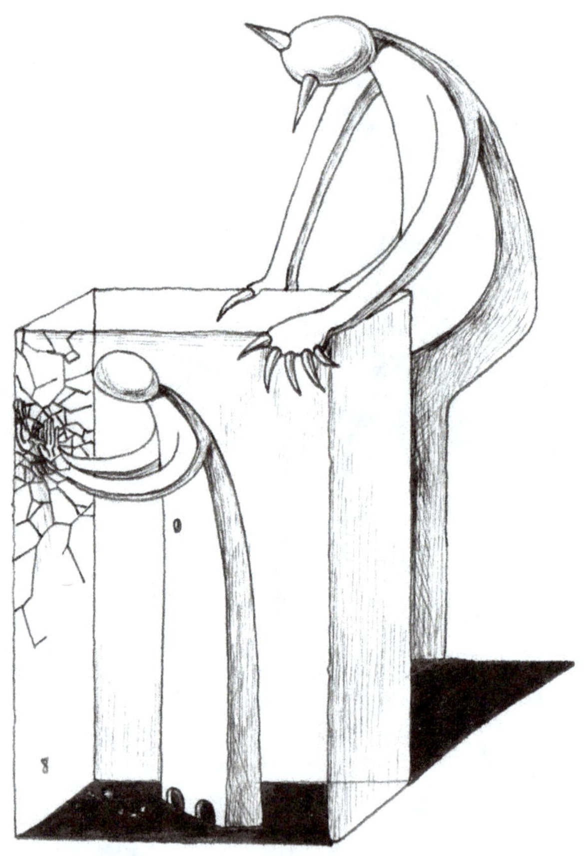

THE ORIGIN OF TROUBLES

Most of our troubles come from the fear of being alone.

THE PING-PONG PLAYERS

People who walk into marriage become ping-pong players in a game. They are far from the crowd and yet cannot be alone.

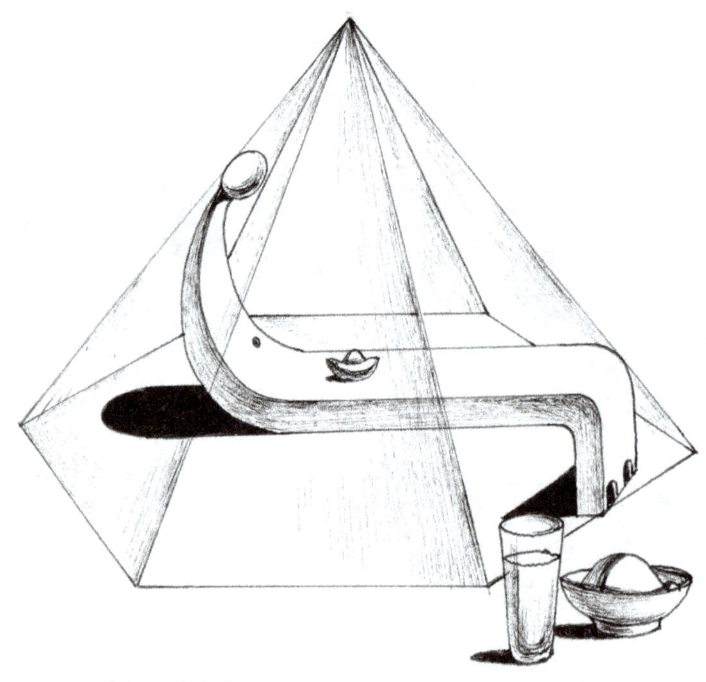

THE PRECIOUS THINGS

The most precious things are often easy to get, such as air and water. What we make the maximum efforts to get often have no practical value, such as a diamond or a reputation.

THE PRIDE

Your pride is already lost when you care about it.

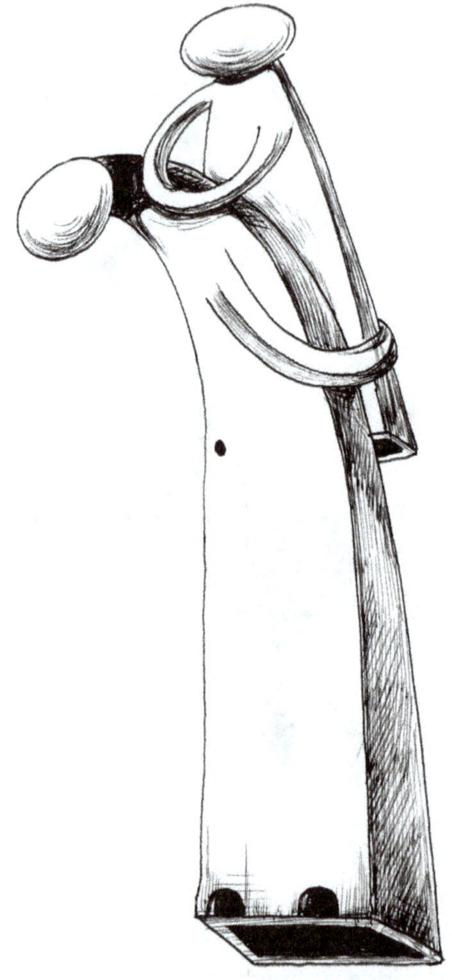

THE REDEMPTION

The devotion of parents to their children is almost like an act of redemption because they deeply know that they brought their children into an imperfect world.

THE REGRETS

The significant regrets in lives are mostly from insignificance mistakes.

THE RESPONSIBILITY

Vulnerability is not an excuse to abandon a fight. We are fine to lose due to deficient ability, but we still absolutely carry a responsibility to level up our enemies' winning.

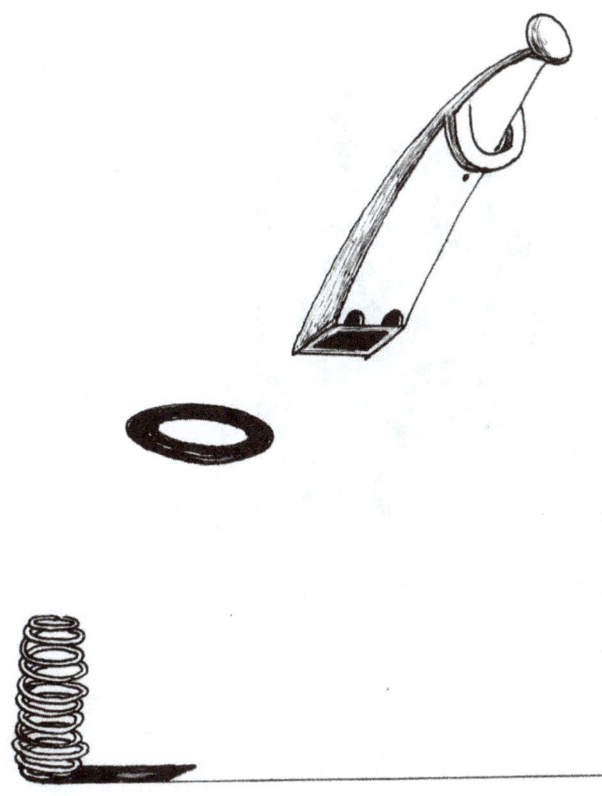

THE RESULT

Spending time to expect a result is exactly the worst result.

THE REVERSED

Every other decades or hundreds of years, the evaluation for a historical figure would be reversed. This is because those who are alive are ill, and the dead ones have no needs to be surprised.

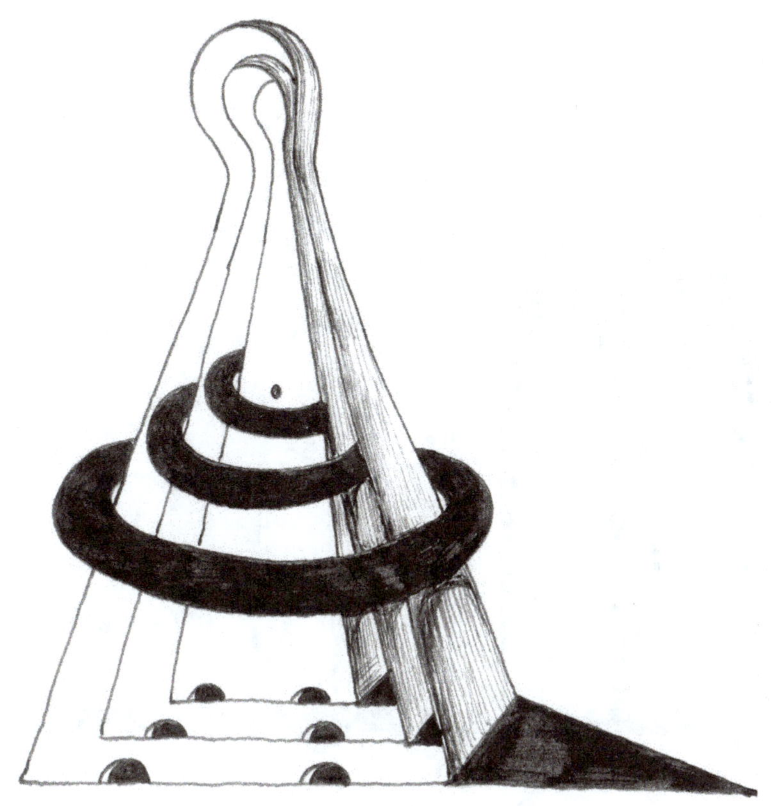

THE ROLE

The role of SCHOOL is to let the kids smash school's windows rather than the residents'. The role of UNIVERSITY is to lock up the young adults that are too easy to be fooled. The role of MARRIAGE is to lock people up for the rest of their lives, whether they have been to university or not.

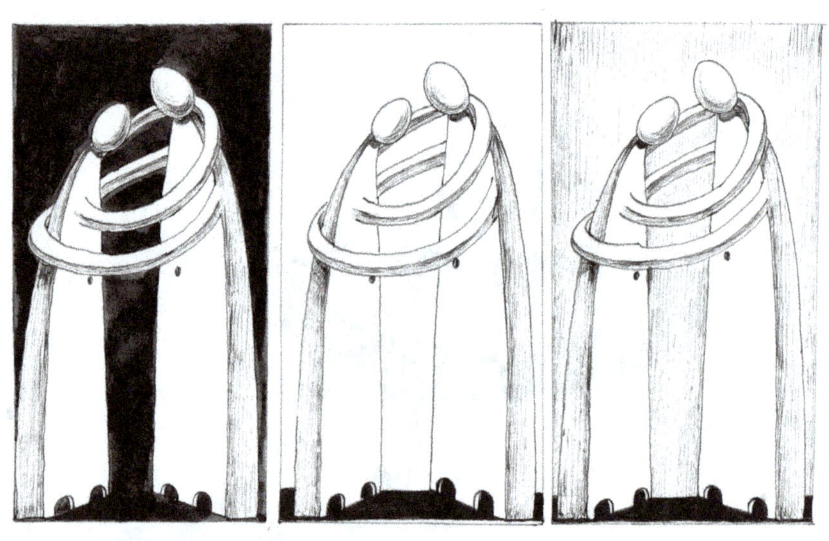

THE SAME

Is everyone's life different? It is surely the same after falling in love.

THE SETBACKS

It is only when you move forward that you feel the bumps. It is only when you experience growth that you encounter setbacks.

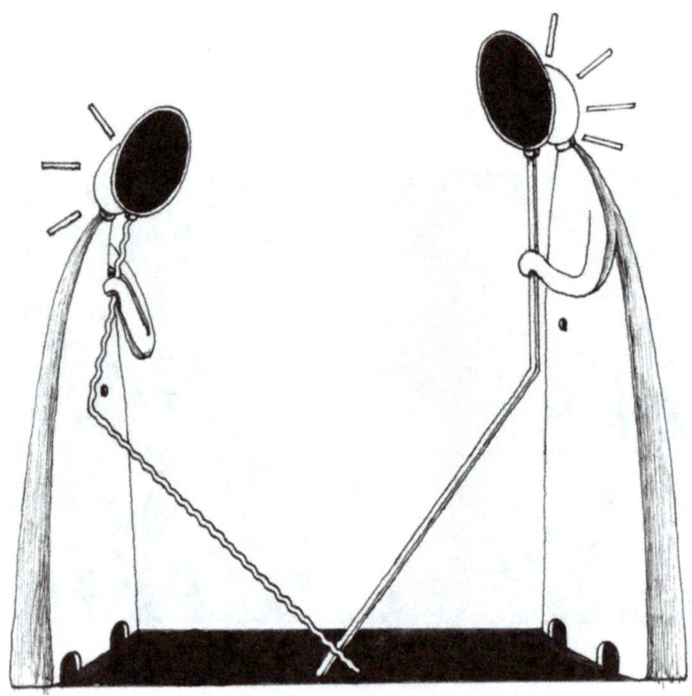

THE SKY GETTING DARK

The sky gets dark because we need to arrange a special time to accomplish things that cannot be done in daylight. As we know, it happens every day.

THE SPEED
Never stop moving is the top speed.

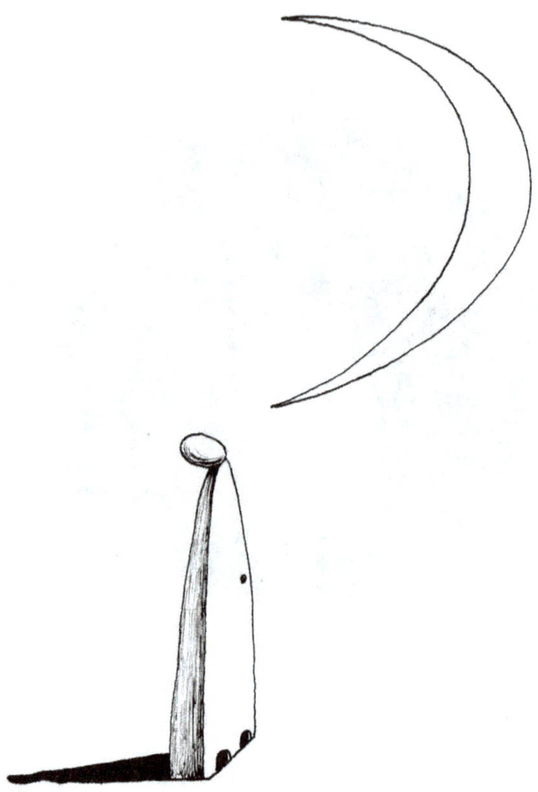

THE STARRY SKY

When human look up into the starry sky, they will most likely come up with the deep thought that the moon is the largest star in the universe.

THE STATUE

When a man's statue is built, it means either that he is died already or he has a firm belief in eternity.

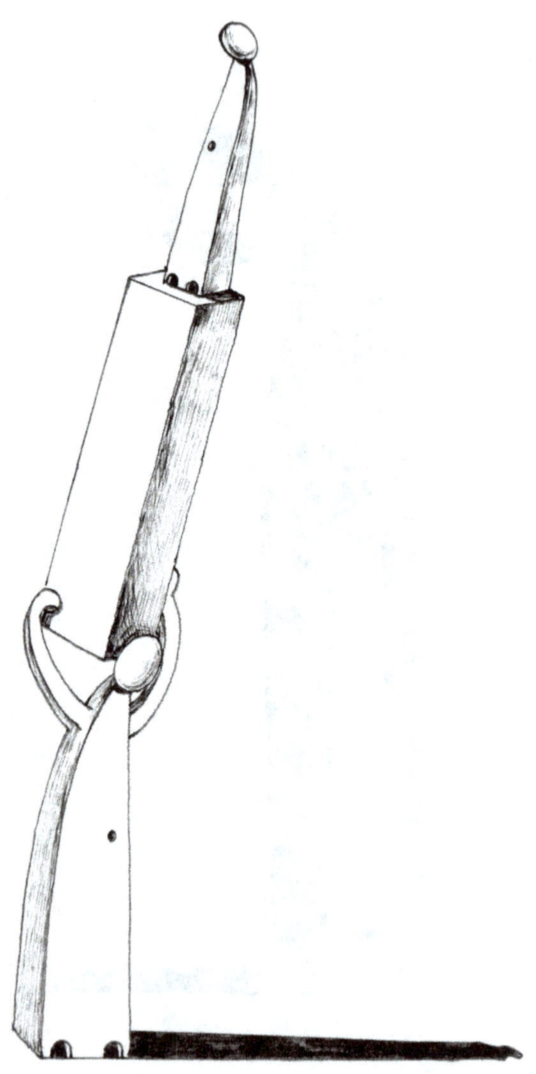

THE SUCCESSES

Most successes are unworthy of their label. The real successes in the eyes of the world are more like failures.

THE SYMPATHY AND JEALOUSY

Suffering together is easy because of sympathy of humanity. Celebrating together is difficult because of jealousy of humanity.

THE TALENTS

People have different talents. Unfortunately, the number of people who identify their talents and the number of people who identify their weaknesses are both quite low.

THE THINGS YOU NEED

Things that you need always belong to someone who does not need them.

THE TOOTHACHE

Toothache is a religion. It makes people appreciate the days without it.

THE TROUBLES

If you still have some free time to be troubled, then your troubles are really nothing.

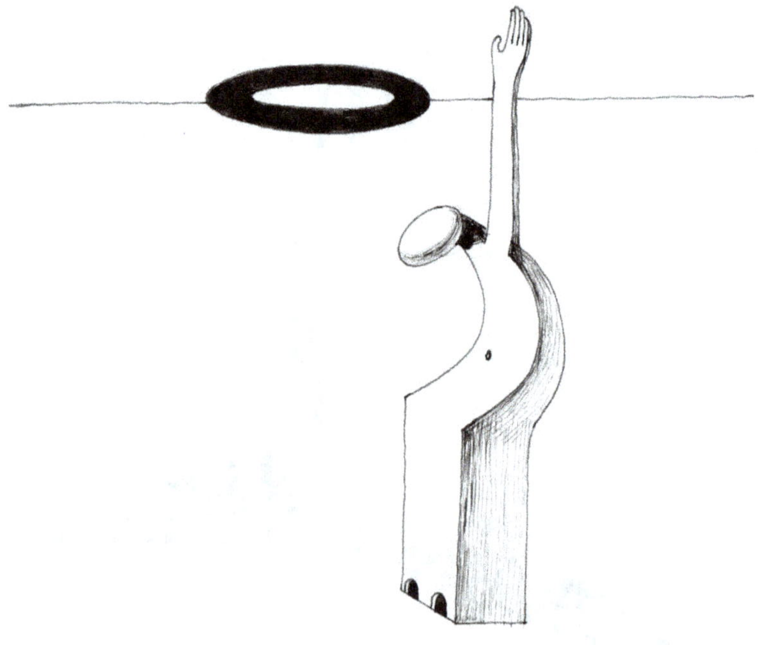

THE TRUTH

The fundamental cause of why we cannot find truth is that it is dynamic but not static.

THE TYRANT

Anyone will become a tyrant if he has supreme power.

THE UNNERVING THING

The most unnerving thing about time is not how fast it is but that it never stops.

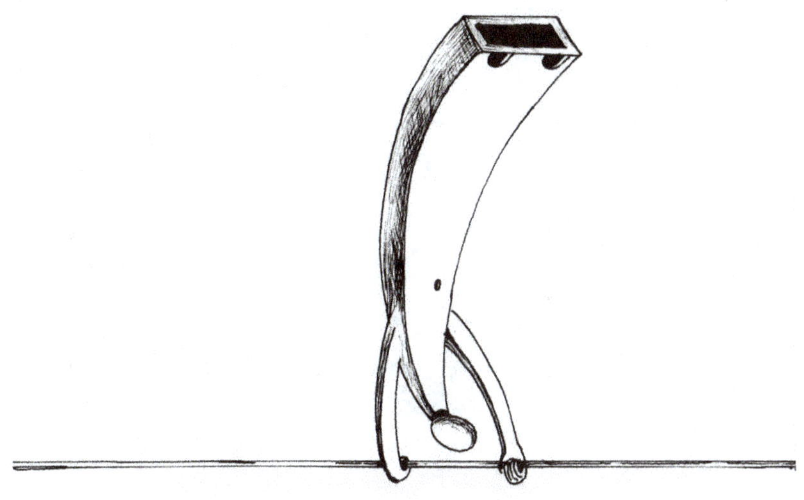

THE VAULTING POLE

An obstacle is the best vaulting pole.

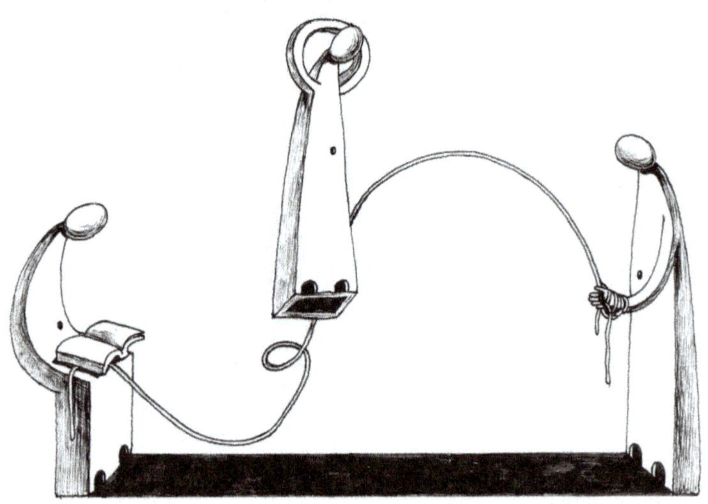

THE WISE MEN

The wise men often look kind of stupid because they are not stupid enough to spend extra time on those meaningless things.

THE YOUTH

The key beauty of youth comes from the unbalance between your ability and ambition. When you are more than ready for the tasks, your life will be boring.

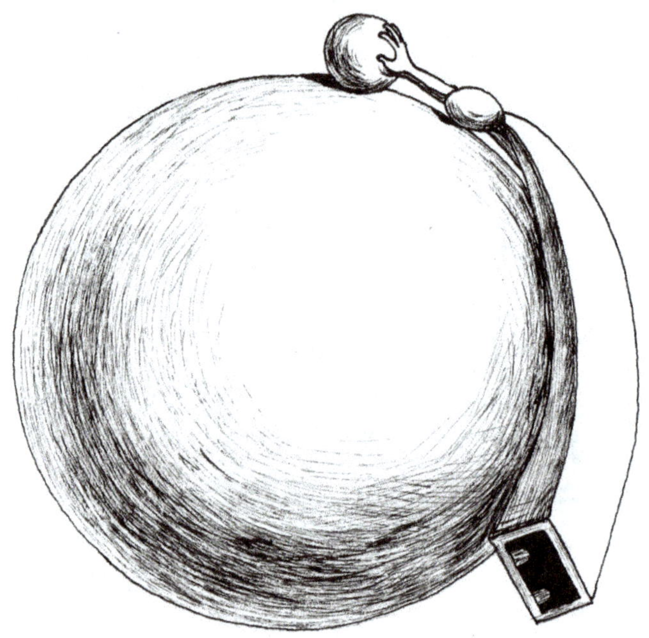

TIME FLIES

Finding some hard work to do is better than sighing for the past. By then, you will complain about how time goes so slowly.

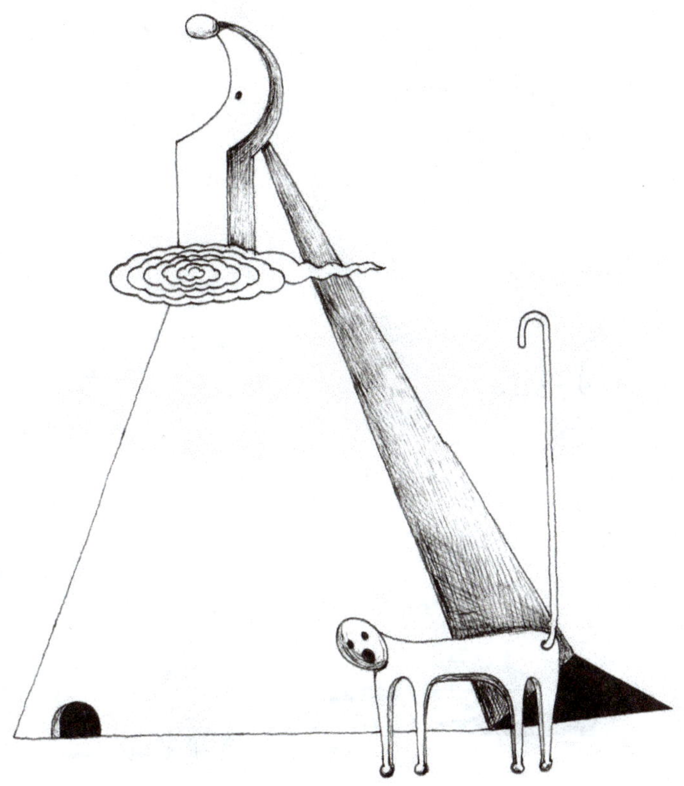

TO BE A HERMIT

It is possible to be a hermit in the mountains, but it is impossible to live a carefree life because the beasts in the mountains are more aggressive than those in the cities.

TO BE STRONG

Pretending to be strong would make you look weaker.

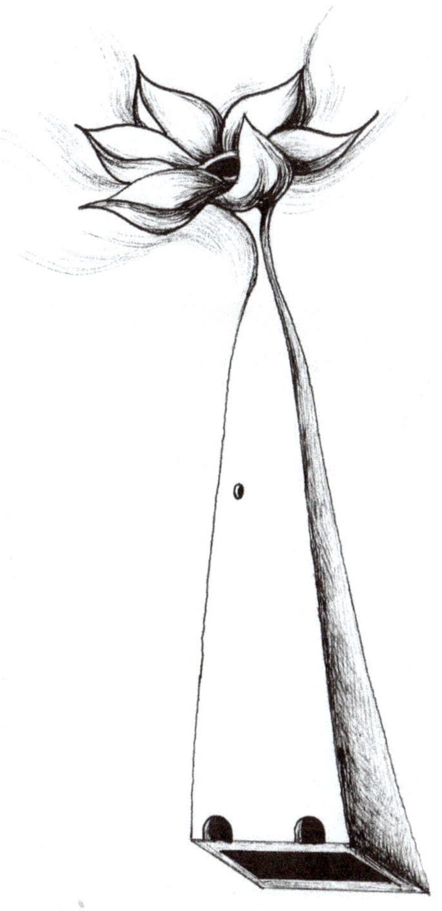

TO BETRAY

Excessive praises of the youth is an act of betrayal for other wonderful periods of life.

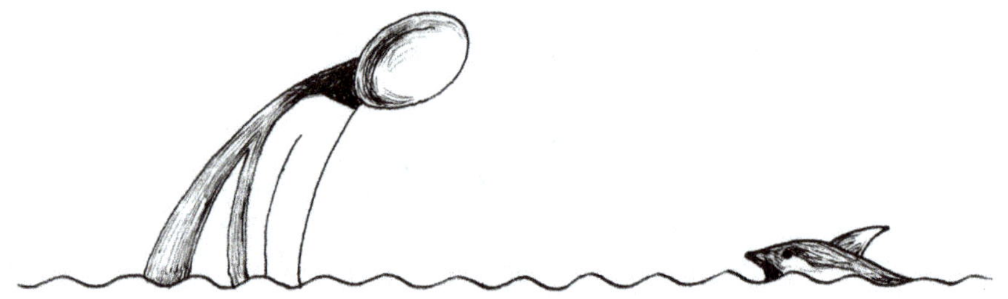

TO BREATHE

Fish can breathe in water because they have no feet to get away from water.

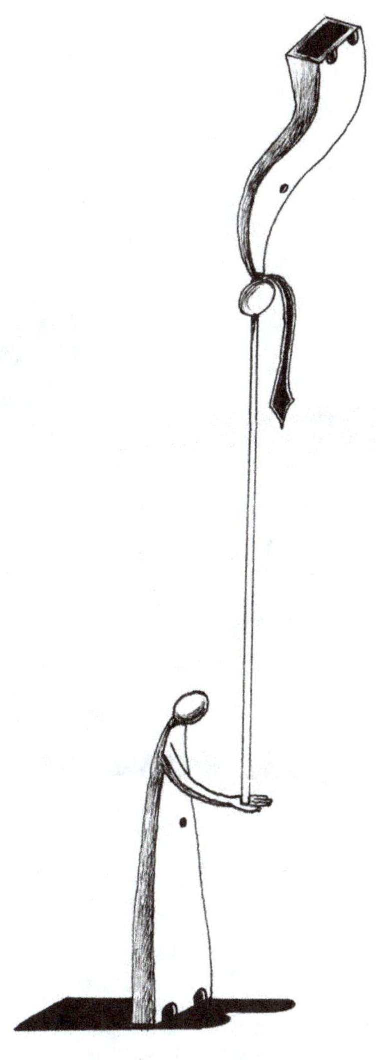

TO CONTROL

The more people try to control others, the more self-control they will lose.

TO CREATE

Wise people generally make up some inconsequential shortcomings of themselves and spread them out for others to laugh at. This is because that wise people understand something: if they not guide the imagination of others, others will create much bigger surprise.

TO DISTORT

The effort to keep your body clean in sludges will eventually distort your mind.

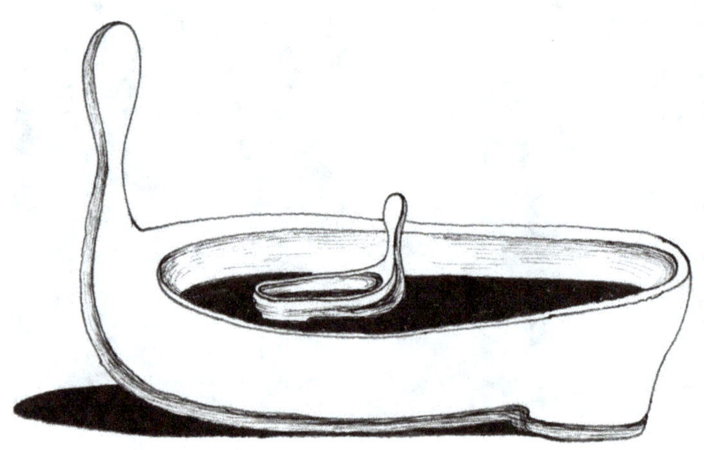

TO FORGIVE

You do not have adequate ability to forgive others until you exhibit strong enough power to defeat them.

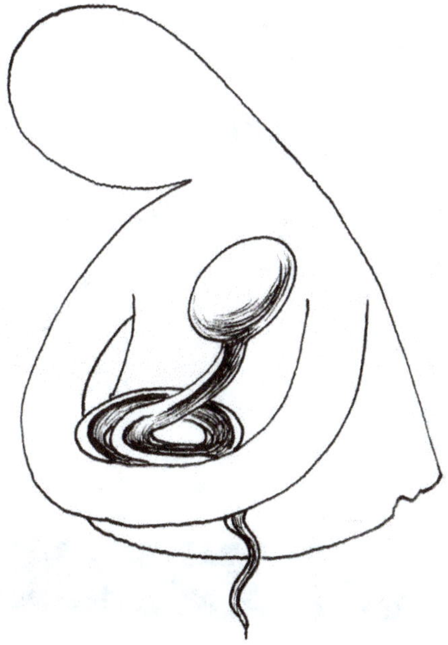

TO HELP

If you offered help to people but never got hurt from them, then they are extremely merciful.

TO JUDGE

The only criterion for a woman to judge a man is that if she loves him.

TO LABOR

Labor can purify your soul more than what meditation can.

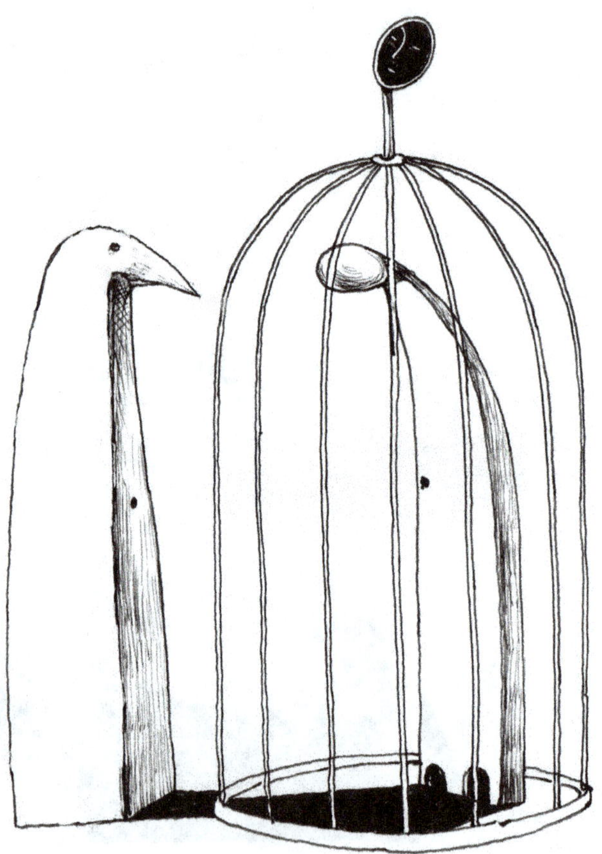

TO LOSE

You will eventually lose what you have caused other people to lose.

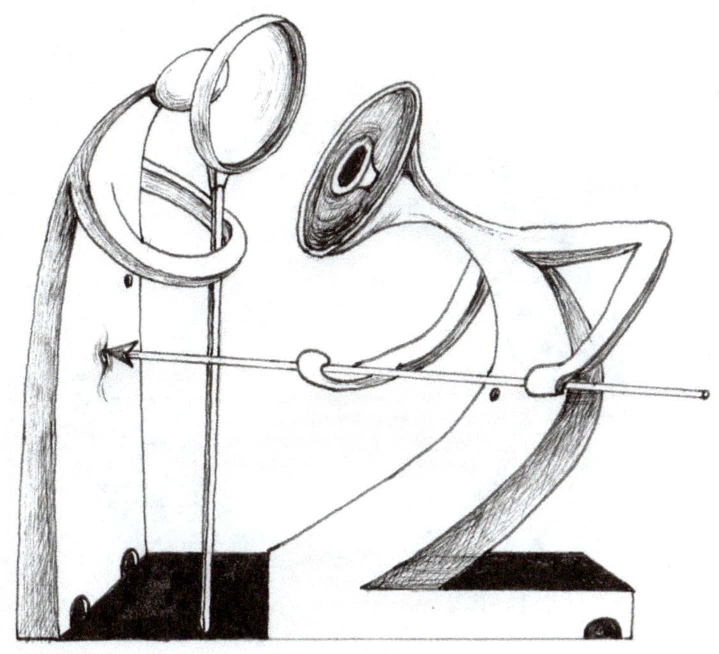

TO LOVE OR HATE

When a woman loves or hates a man, it is not because of his actions but his words.

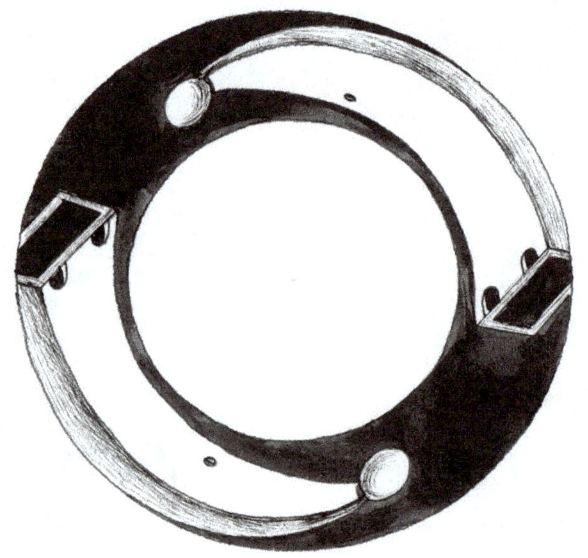

TO REIN

We can neither rein over our body nor our heart, much less giving up the two attempts.

TO RESPECT

Respecting others is not to surrender in humiliation but to dignity yourself.

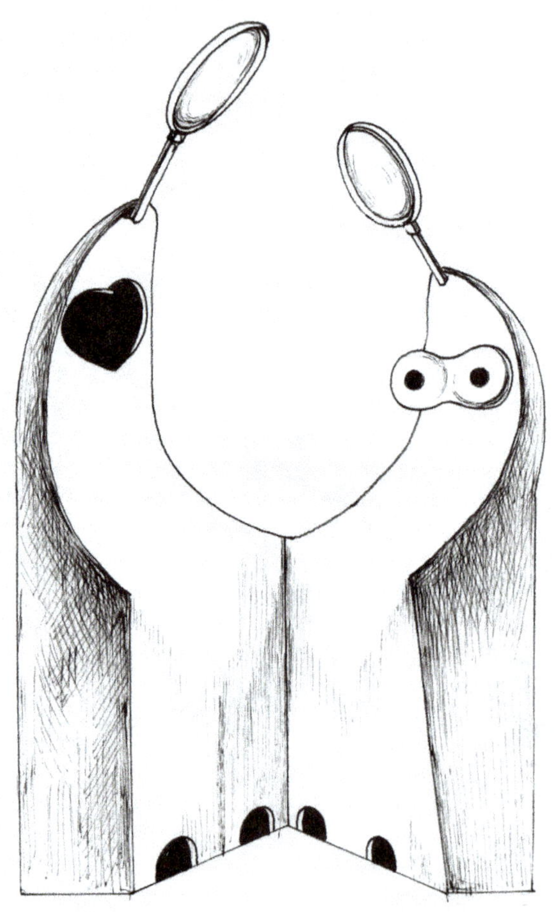

TO SEE

A woman always wants to see a man's heart, but a man just wants to see a woman's breasts.

TO SPECULATE

If you cannot even read the thoughts of the woman in your arms, how can you possibly speculate the ancient stories that have been countlessly paraphrased.

TO STAY SILENT

Only a man who is ready to explode will be willing to stay silent.

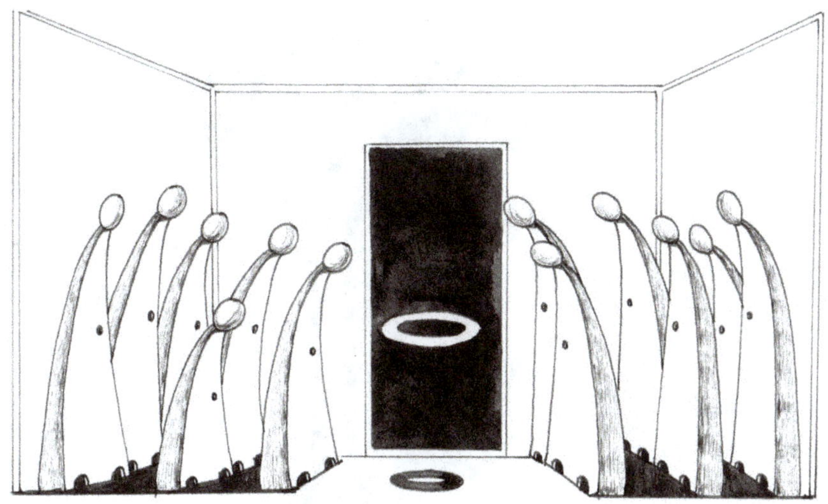

TO THINK AS A THINKER

When a thinker starts to think as a thinker, there are no thoughts produced anymore.

TO WASTE

Peoples never waste time. They would only be wasted by time.

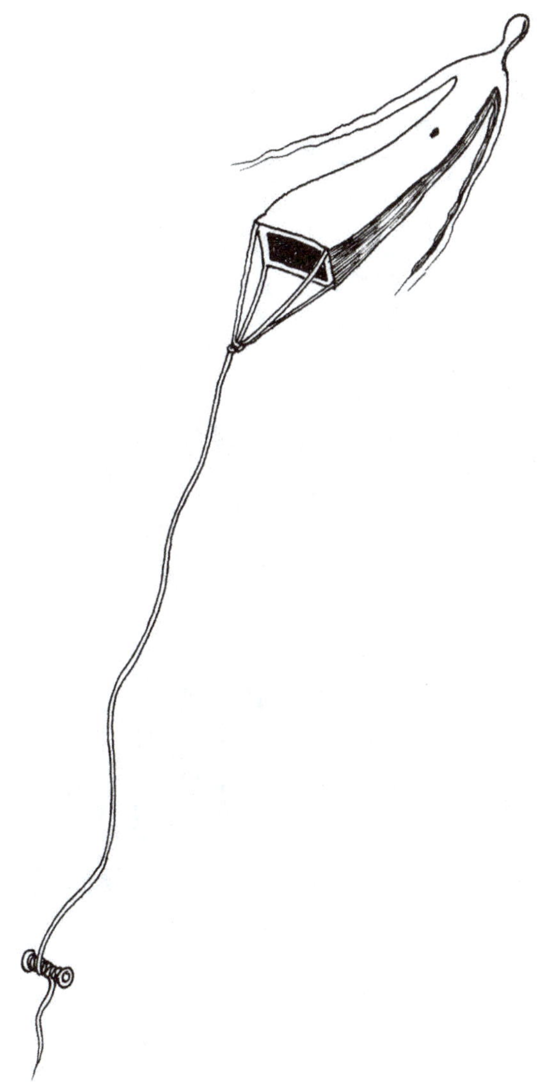

TRAVELING ROUND THE WORLD

A lot of people constantly talk about their dream of traveling around the world. However, they have even not yet appreciated the scenery outside of their windows.

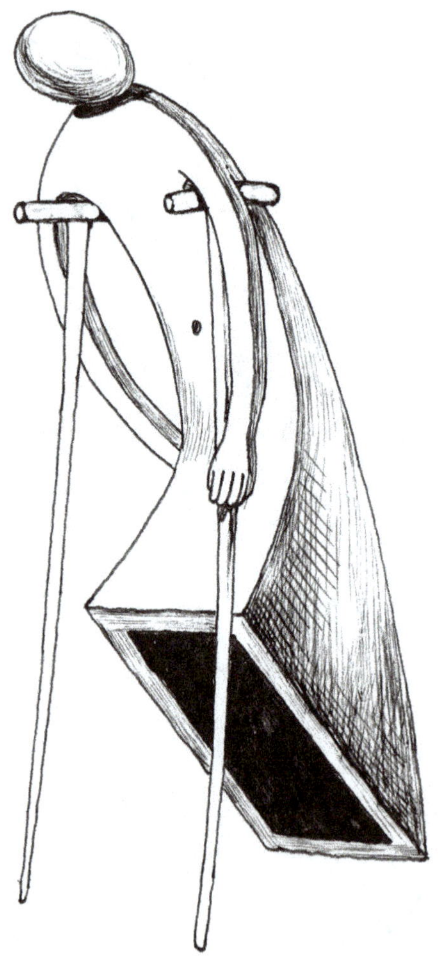

UNDERSTANDING

Only a person who has no legs can truly understand the joy of having hands.

US

How can we let ourselves realize that we are only a part of nature but not its master?

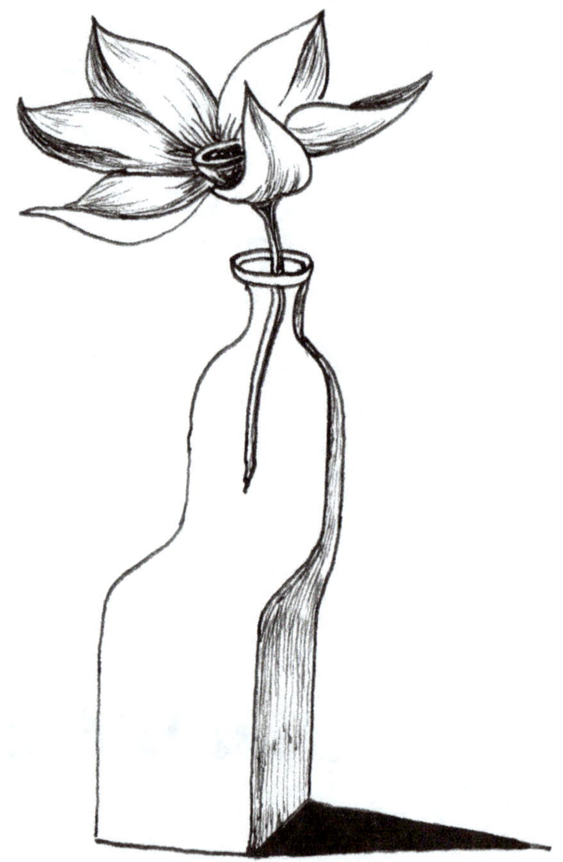

VALUE

If we closely inspect the real value of the things we own, we will find that many people actually have no possessions.

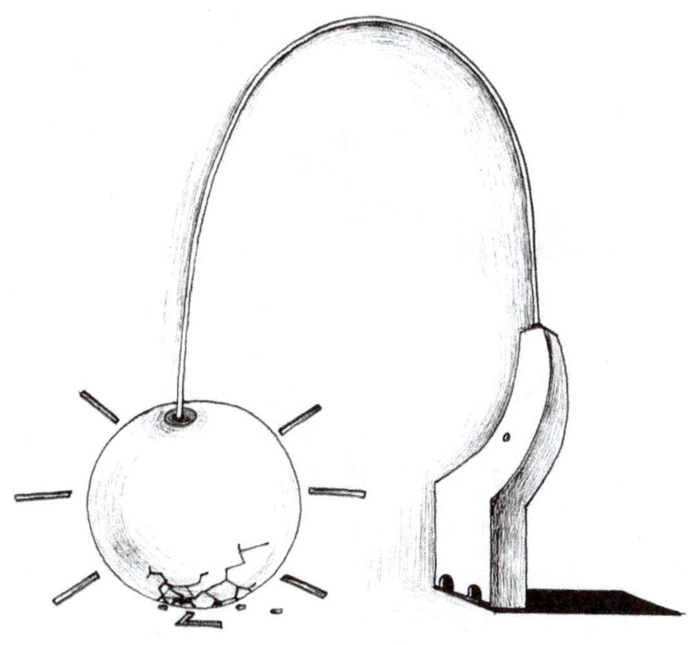

VANITY

Vanity is a shortcut to shame.

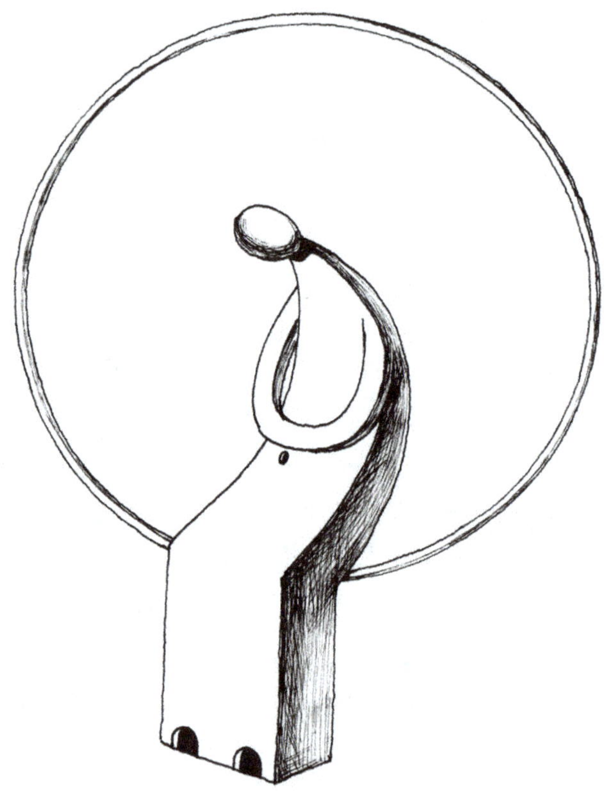

WAITING

WAITING means pausing for a while on your journey and imagining the destination to come to you.

WITH FOOD

Our lives become pathetic and sad because we cannot live without food.

The Words of Yemen Chen 2018 English 1st Edition

ISBN13: 978-1-7328459-6-1
ISBN: 1-7328459-6-4
LCCN: 2018913594

Los Angeles: Losget Press, 2018
www.losget.com
E-mail: contact@losget.com

www.ingramcontent.com/pod-product-compliance
Lightning Source LLC
Chambersburg PA
CBHW051518030726
47592CB00006B/2327

* 9 7 8 1 7 3 2 8 4 5 9 6 1 *